"*Gentle and Lowly* comes from the pen of someone who has not just profited from reading the Puritans—but who, more importantly, has read the Bible under their tutelage. One short book can never be enough to convey all the glory of the character of Christ, but this book deftly unpacks something we often overlook: Christ is meek and lowly in heart and gives rest to those who labor and are burdened. Written with pastoral gentleness and quiet beauty, it teases out what twenty biblical texts contribute to this portrait of the heart of Christ, all of it brought together to bring comfort, strength, and rest to believers."

> **D. A. Carson,** Emeritus Professor of New Testament, Trinity
> Evangelical Divinity School; Cofounder, The Gospel Coalition

"In this timely work, Dane Ortlund directs our attention back to the person of Jesus. Centered on the Scriptures and drawing upon the best of the Puritan tradition, Ortlund helps us see the heart of God as it is revealed to us in Christ. He reminds us not only of Jesus's promises of rest and comfort, but of the Bible's vision of Jesus: a kind and gracious King."

> **Russell Moore,** President, The Ethics & Religious Liberty
> Commission of the Southern Baptist Convention

"The title of this book immediately evoked within me a sense of longing, hope, and gratitude. The message it contains is a balm for every heart that feels pierced by sin or sorrow—whether from within or without. It is an invitation to experience the sweet consolations of a Savior who moves toward us with tenderness and grace, when we know we deserve just the opposite from him."

> **Nancy DeMoss Wolgemuth,** author; Teacher and Host, *Revive*
> *Our Hearts*

"My life has been transformed by the beautiful, staggering truths in this book. Dane Ortlund lifts our eyes to see Christ's compassion-filled heart for sinners and sufferers, proving that Jesus is no reluctant savior but one who delights in showing his mercy. For any feeling bruised, weary, or empty, this is the balm for you."

> **Michael Reeves,** President and Professor of Theology, Union School of
> Theology, Oxford, UK

"On the rough, rocky, and often dark path between the 'already' and the 'not yet,' there is nothing your weary heart needs more than to know the beauty of the heart of Jesus. It is that beauty that alone has the power to overwhelm all the ugly you will encounter along the way. I have read no book that more carefully, thoroughly, and tenderly displays Christ's heart than what Dane Ortlund has written. As if I was listening to a great symphony, I was moved in different ways in different passages but left each feeling hugely blessed to know that what was being described was the heart of my Savior, my Lord, my Friend, and my Redeemer. I can't think of anyone in the family of God who wouldn't be greatly helped by spending time seeing the heart of Jesus through the eyes of such a gifted guide as Ortlund."

Paul David Tripp, President, Paul Tripp Ministries; author, *New Morning Mercies* and *My Heart Cries Out*

"The Puritans breathed Christ-centered practices: they embraced the Bible as a lifeline, exercised it like a muscle, and relied upon it like a bulletproof vest. They knew how to hate their sin without hating themselves because they understood that Christ's grace is an ever-present person, a person who understands our situation and our needs better than we do. They understood that we suffer because of sin. Dane Ortlund masterfully handles a treasure trove of Puritan wisdom and deftly presents it to the Christian reader. Read this book and pray that the Holy Spirit reveals Christ to you as the Puritans understood him, and you will be refreshed to understand God's grace in a whole new way."

Rosaria Butterfield, Former Professor of English, Syracuse University; author, *The Gospel Comes with a House Key*

"'He is so strong that he can afford to be gentle.' That old movie line is more than a throwaway sentiment when we consider the theological precision and pastoral heart of Dane Ortlund describing God's heart toward those who are weak, weary, sin-sick, and despairing. The insights of *Gentle and Lowly* are truly a river of mercy flowing from the throne of God, through great pastors of the past, and into precious and powerful ministry for today."

Bryan Chapell, Senior Pastor, Grace Presbyterian Church, Peoria, Illinois

"Only a few pages in I started to realize how unusual and essential this book is—it is an exposition of the very heart of Christ. The result is a book that astonishes us with the sheer abundance and capacity of his love for us. Breathtaking and healing in equal measure, it is already one of the best books I've read."

Sam Allberry, Apologist and Speaker, author, *7 Myths about Singleness*

"Dane Ortlund writes about what seems too good to be true—the Lord delights to show mercy to you and to me—so he works very carefully through key texts and enlists the help of saints past. I was persuaded, and I look forward to being persuaded again and again."

Ed Welch, Counselor and Faculty Member, Christian Counseling & Educational Foundation

"Dane Ortlund leads us into the very heart of God incarnate—not only what Jesus did for us, but how he *feels* toward us. That's right: feels toward us. Anchored in Scripture and drawing on the Puritan Thomas Goodwin, this book is medicine for broken hearts."

Michael Horton, J. Gresham Machen Professor of Systematic Theology and Apologetics, Westminster Seminary California

"Dane Ortlund helps us rediscover the heart of Jesus that is the very heart of the gospel. This delightful book opens up the sheer immensity of Jesus's tender love for us. As you immerse yourself in Christ's very heart, you'll find your own heart warmed at the fire of the love of God. Ortlund opens up a neglected theme among the Puritans (in bite-sized chunks that won't overwhelm you), where you'll discover their grasp of the beauty of Jesus's love. Your soul needs this book. I highly recommend it."

Paul E. Miller, author, *A Praying Life* and *J-Curve: Dying and Rising with Jesus in Everyday Life*

GENTLE

— *and* —

LOWLY

The Heart of Christ for
Sinners and Sufferers

Dane Ortlund

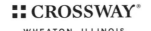

WHEATON, ILLINOIS

Cover design: Jordan Singer

Cover image: Photo © Christie's Images / Bridgeman Images

First printing 2020

Printed in the United States of America

Scripture quotations are from the ESV® Bible (The Holy Bible, English Standard Version®), copyright © 2001 by Crossway, a publishing ministry of Good News Publishers. Used by permission. All rights reserved.

Scripture quotations marked CEB are taken from the Common English Bible®, copyright © 2011. Used by permission. All rights reserved.

Scripture quotations marked CSB are from the Christian Standard Bible. Copyright © 2017 by Holman Bible Publishers. Used by permission. Christian Standard Bible®, and CSB® are federally registered trademarks of Holman Bible Publishers. All rights reserved.

Scripture quotations marked GNB are from the *Good News Bible* © 1994 published by the Bible Societies/HarperCollins Publishers Ltd., *UK Good News Bible* © by American Bible Society 1966, 1971, 1976, 1992. Used with permission.

Scripture quotations marked KJV are from the *King James Version* of the Bible.

Scripture quotations marked NASB are from *The New American Standard Bible*®. Copyright © The Lockman Foundation 1960, 1962, 1963, 1968, 1971, 1972, 1973, 1975, 1977, 1995. Used by permission.

Scripture quotations marked NET are from *The NET Bible*® copyright © 2003 by Biblical Studies Press, L.L.C. www.netbible.com. All rights reserved. Quoted by permission.

Scripture references marked NIV are taken from The Holy Bible, New International Version®, NIV®. Copyright © 1973, 1978, 1984, 2011 by Biblica, Inc.™ Used by permission. All rights reserved worldwide.

Scripture references marked NKJV are from *The New King James Version*. Copyright © 1982, Thomas Nelson, Inc. Used by permission.

Scripture references marked RSV are from *The Revised Standard Version*. Copyright © 1946, 1952, 1971, 1973 by the Division of Christian Education of the National Council of the Churches of Christ in the U.S.A.

All emphases in Scripture quotations have been added by the author.

Trade paperback ISBN: 978-1-4335-6613-4
ePub ISBN: 978-1-4335-6616-5
PDF ISBN: 978-1-4335-6614-1
Mobipocket ISBN: 978-1-4335-6615-8

Library of Congress Cataloging-in-Publication Data

Names: Ortlund, Dane Calvin, author.
Title: Gentle and lowly : the heart of Christ for sinners and sufferers / Dane Ortlund.
Description: Wheaton : Crossway, 2020. | Includes bibliographical references and index.
Identifiers: LCCN 2019025868 (print) | LCCN 2019025869 (ebook) | ISBN 9781433566134 (hardcover) | ISBN 9781433566141 (pdf) | ISBN 9781433566158 (mobi) | ISBN 9781433566165 (epub)
Subjects: LCSH: God (Christianity)—Mercy. | God (Christianity)–Love. | Suffering of God. | Jesus Christ.
Classification: LCC BT153.M4 O78 2020 (print) | LCC BT153.M4 (ebook) | DDC 231.7–dc23
LC record available at https://lccn.loc.gov/2019025868
LC ebook record available at https://lccn.loc.gov/2019025869

Crossway is a publishing ministry of Good News Publishers.

To Hope
Luke 18:16

Fatherlike he tends and spares us
Well our feeble frame he knows
In his hand he gently bears us
Rescues us from all our foes

H. F. LYTE, 1834

Contents

Introduction

THIS IS A BOOK ABOUT the heart of Christ. Who is he? Who is he *really*? What is most natural to him? What ignites within him most immediately as he moves toward sinners and sufferers? What flows out most freely, most instinctively? Who *is* he?

This book is written for the discouraged, the frustrated, the weary, the disenchanted, the cynical, the empty. Those running on fumes. Those whose Christian lives feel like constantly running up a descending escalator. Those of us who find ourselves thinking: "How could I mess up that bad—again?" It is for that increasing suspicion that God's patience with us is wearing thin. For those of us who know God loves us but suspect we have deeply disappointed him. Who have told others of the love of Christ yet wonder if—as for us—he harbors mild resentment. Who wonder if we have shipwrecked our lives beyond what can be repaired. Who are convinced we've permanently diminished our usefulness to the Lord. Who have been swept off our feet by perplexing pain and are wondering how we can keep living under such numbing darkness. Who look at our lives and know how to interpret the data only by concluding that God is fundamentally parsimonious.

It is written, in other words, for normal Christians. In short, it is for sinners and sufferers. How does Jesus feel about them?

This may already raise some eyebrows. Are we overly humanizing Jesus, talking about his feelings this way? From another angle, how does the heart of Christ relate to the doctrine of the Trinity—does Christ relate to us differently than the Father or the Spirit relates to us? Or are we already out of proportion if we ask what is most central to who Christ is? And how does his heart relate to his wrath? Yet again, how does Christ's heart fit with what we find in the Old Testament and its portrait of God?

These questions are not only legitimate but necessary. So we will proceed with theological care. But the safest way to theological fidelity is sticking close to the biblical text. And we are simply going to ask what the Bible says about the heart of Christ and consider the glory of his heart for our own up-and-down lives.

But we are neither the first nor the smartest to read the Bible. Throughout the history of the church God has raised up uniquely gifted and insightful teachers to walk the rest of us into the green pastures and still waters of who God in Christ is. One particularly concentrated period of history in which God provided penetrating Bible teachers was 1600s England and the age of the Puritans. This book on Christ's heart would not exist if I had not stumbled upon the Puritans and especially Thomas Goodwin. It is Goodwin more than anyone who has opened my eyes to who God in Christ is, most naturally and easily, for fickle sinners. But Goodwin and the others raised in this book such as Sibbes and Bunyan are channels, not sources. The Bible is the source. They're just showing us with particular clarity and insight what the Bible has been telling us all along about who God actually is.

And so the strategy of this book will simply be to take either a Bible passage or a bit of teaching from the Puritans or others and consider what is being said about the heart of God and of Christ. We will consider the prophets Isaiah and Jeremiah, the apostles John and Paul, the Puritans Goodwin and Sibbes and Bunyan and Owen, and others such as Edwards and Spurgeon and Warfield and open ourselves up to what they tell us about the heart of God and the heart of Christ. The controlling question is: Who *is* he? There will be a fairly natural progression through the book from chapter to chapter, though not so much as a logically building argument but rather looking at the single diamond of Christ's heart from many different angles.

It is one thing to ask what Christ has done. And there are many sound books on this. Consider Stott's *The Cross of Christ;*[1] or Jeffery, Ovey, and Sach's *Pierced for Our Transgressions;*[2] or Macleod's *Christ Crucified;*[3] or Packer's seminal 1974 article;[4] or a dozen other solid historical or contemporary treatments. We are not focusing centrally on what Christ has done. We are considering who he is. The two matters are bound up together and indeed interdependent. But they are distinct. The gospel offers us not only legal exoneration—inviolably precious truth!—it also sweeps us into Christ's very heart. You might know that Christ died and rose again on your behalf to

---

1 John R. W. Stott, *The Cross of Christ* (Downers Grove, IL: InterVarsity Press, 1986).
2 Steve Jeffery, Michael Ovey, and Andrew Sach, *Pierced for Our Transgressions: Recovering the Glory of Penal Substitution* (Wheaton, IL: Crossway, 2007).
3 Donald Macleod, *Christ Crucified: Understanding the Atonement* (Downers Grove, IL: InterVarsity Press, 2014).
4 J. I. Packer, "What Did the Cross Achieve? The Logic of Penal Substitution," *Tyndale Bulletin* 25 (1974): 3–45.

rinse you clean of all your sin; but do you know his deepest heart for you? Do you live with an awareness not only of his atoning work for your sinfulness but also of his longing heart amid your sinfulness?

A wife may tell you much about her husband—his height, his eye color, his eating habits, his education, his job, his handiness around the house, his best friend, his hobbies, his Myers-Briggs personality profile, his favorite sports team. But what can she say to communicate his knowing gaze across the table over a dinner at their favorite restaurant? That look that reflects years of ever-deepening friendship, thousands of conversations and arguments through which they have safely come, a time-ripened settling into the assurance of embrace, come what may? That glance that speaks in a moment his loving protection more clearly than a thousand words? In short, what can she say to communicate to another her husband's *heart* for her?

It is one thing to describe what your husband says and does and looks like. It is something else, something deeper and more real, to describe his heart for you.

So with Christ. It is one thing to know the doctrines of the incarnation and the atonement and a hundred other vital doctrines. It is another, more searching matter to know his heart for you.

Who is he?

1

His Very Heart

I am gentle and lowly in heart.
MATTHEW 11:29

MY DAD POINTED OUT TO ME something that Charles Spurgeon pointed out to him. In the four Gospel accounts given to us in Matthew, Mark, Luke, and John—eighty-nine chapters of biblical text—there's only one place where Jesus tells us about his own heart.

We learn much in the four Gospels about Christ's teaching. We read of his birth, his ministry, and his disciples. We are told of his travels and prayer habits. We find lengthy speeches and repeated objections by his hearers, prompting further teaching. We learn of the way he understood himself to fulfill the whole Old Testament. And we learn in all four accounts of his unjust arrest and shameful death and astonishing resurrection. Consider the thousands of pages that have been written by theologians over the past two thousand years on all these things.

But in only one place—perhaps the most wonderful words ever uttered by human lips—do we hear Jesus himself open up to us his very heart:

> Come to me, all who labor and are heavy laden, and I will give you rest. Take my yoke upon you, and learn from me, for I am gentle and lowly in heart, and you will find rest for your souls. For my yoke is easy, and my burden is light. (Matt. 11:28–30)[1]

In the one place in the Bible where the Son of God pulls back the veil and lets us peer way down into the core of who he is, we are not told that he is "austere and demanding in heart." We are not told that he is "exalted and dignified in heart." We are not even told that he is "joyful and generous in heart." Letting Jesus set the terms, his surprising claim is that he is "gentle and lowly in heart."

One thing to get straight right from the start is that when the Bible speaks of the heart, whether Old Testament or New, it is not speaking of our emotional life only but of the central animating center of all we do. It is what gets us out of bed in the morning and what we daydream about as we drift off to sleep. It is our motivation headquarters. The heart, in biblical terms, is not part of who we are but the center of who we are. Our heart is what defines and directs us. That is why Solomon tells us to "keep [the] heart with all vigilance, for from it flows the springs of life" (Prov. 4:23).[2] The

---

1 Matt. 11:29 was the German Reformer Philip Melanchthon's favorite verse in the Bible. Herman Bavinck, "John Calvin: A Lecture on the Occasion of His 400th Birthday," trans. John Bolt, *The Bavinck Review* 1 (2010): 62.

2 Another Puritan, John Flavel, devoted a whole treatise to this verse and to strategies to maintain the heart: John Flavel, *Keeping the Heart: How to Maintain Your Love for God* (Fearn, Scotland: Christian Focus, 2012).

heart is a matter of life. It is what makes us the human being each of us is. The heart drives all we do. It is who we are.[3]

And when Jesus tells us what animates him most deeply, what is most true of him—when he exposes the innermost recesses of his being—what we find there is: gentle and lowly.

Who could ever have thought up such a Savior?

———

"I am gentle . . ."

The Greek word translated "gentle" here occurs just three other times in the New Testament: in the first beatitude, that "the *meek*" will inherit the earth (Matt. 5:5); in the prophecy in Matthew 21:5 (quoting Zech. 9:9) that Jesus the king "is coming to you, *humble*, and mounted on a donkey"; and in Peter's encouragement to wives to nurture more than anything else "the hidden person of the heart with the imperishable beauty of a *gentle* and quiet spirit" (1 Pet. 3:4). Meek. Humble. Gentle. Jesus is not trigger-happy. Not harsh, reactionary, easily exasperated. He is the most understanding person in the universe. The posture most natural to him is not a pointed finger but open arms.

". . . and lowly . . ."

The meaning of the word "lowly" overlaps with that of "gentle," together communicating a single reality about Jesus's heart. This specific word *lowly* is generally translated "humble" in the New

---

3   An excellent treatment on the Bible's teaching on the heart along these lines is Craig Troxel, *With All Your Heart: Orienting Your Mind, Desires, and Will toward Christ* (Wheaton, IL: Crossway, 2020).

Testament, such as in James 4:6: "God opposes the proud but gives grace to the *humble*." But typically throughout the New Testament this Greek word refers not to humility as a virtue but to humility in the sense of destitution or being thrust downward by life circumstance (which is also how this Greek word is generally used throughout the Greek versions of the Old Testament, especially in the psalms). In Mary's song while pregnant with Jesus, for example, this word is used to speak of the way God exalts those who are "of humble estate" (Luke 1:52). Paul uses the word when he tells us to "not be haughty, but associate with the *lowly*" (Rom. 12:16), referring to the socially unimpressive, those who are not the life of the party but rather cause the host to cringe when they show up.

The point in saying that Jesus is lowly is that he is *accessible*. For all his resplendent glory and dazzling holiness, his supreme uniqueness and otherness, no one in human history has ever been more approachable than Jesus Christ. No prerequisites. No hoops to jump through. Warfield, commenting on Matthew 11:29, wrote: "No impression was left by his life-manifestation more deeply imprinted upon the consciousness of his followers than that of the noble humility of his bearing."[4] The minimum bar to be enfolded into the embrace of Jesus is simply: open yourself up to him. It is all he needs. Indeed, it is the only thing he works with. Verse 28 of our passage in Matthew 11 tells us explicitly who qualifies for fellowship with Jesus: "all who labor and are heavy laden." You don't need to unburden or collect yourself and then come to Jesus. Your very burden is what qualifies you to come. No payment is required; he

4 B. B. Warfield, *The Person and Work of Christ* (Oxford, UK: Benediction Classics, 2015), 140.

says, "I will *give* you rest." His rest is gift, not transaction. Whether you are actively working hard to crowbar your life into smoothness ("labor") or passively finding yourself weighed down by something outside your control ("heavy laden"), Jesus Christ's desire that you find rest, that you come in out of the storm, outstrips even your own.

"Gentle and lowly." This, according to his own testimony, is Christ's very heart. This is who he is. Tender. Open. Welcoming. Accommodating. Understanding. Willing. *If we are asked to say only one thing about who Jesus is, we would be honoring Jesus's own teaching if our answer is, gentle and lowly.*

If Jesus hosted his own personal website, the most prominent line of the "About Me" dropdown would read: GENTLE AND LOWLY IN HEART.

This is not who he is to everyone, indiscriminately. This is who he is for those who come to him, who take his yoke upon them, who cry to him for help. The paragraph before these words from Jesus gives us a picture of how Jesus handles the impenitent: "Woe to you, Chorazin! Woe to you, Bethsaida! . . . I tell you that it will be more tolerable on the day of judgment for the land of Sodom than for you" (Matt. 11:21, 24). "Gentle and lowly" does not mean "mushy and frothy."

But for the penitent, his heart of gentle embrace is never out-matched by our sins and foibles and insecurities and doubts and anxieties and failures. For lowly gentleness is not one way Jesus occasionally acts toward others. Gentleness is who he is. It is his heart. He can't un-gentle himself toward his own any more than you or I can change our eye color. It's who we are.

The Christian life is inescapably one of toil and labor (1 Cor. 15:10; Phil. 2:12–13; Col. 1:29). Jesus himself made this clear in this very Gospel (Matt. 5:19–20; 18:8–9). His promise here in Matthew 11 is "rest for your souls," not "rest for your bodies." But all Christian toil flows from fellowship with a living Christ whose transcending, defining reality is: gentle and lowly. He astounds and sustains us with his endless kindness. Only as we walk ever deeper into this tender kindness can we live the Christian life as the New Testament calls us to. Only as we drink down the kindness of the heart of Christ will we leave in our wake, everywhere we go, the aroma of heaven, and die one day having startled the world with glimpses of a divine kindness too great to be boxed in by what we deserve.

That notion of kindness is right here in our passage. The word translated "easy" in his statement, "My yoke is easy," needs to be carefully understood. Jesus is not saying life is free of pain or hardship. This is the same word elsewhere translated "kind"—as in, for example, Ephesians 4:32: "Be *kind* to one another, tenderhearted" (also Rom. 2:4). Consider what Jesus is saying. A yoke is the heavy crossbar laid on oxen to force them to drag farming equipment through the field. Jesus is using a kind of irony, saying that the yoke laid on his disciples is a nonyoke. For it is a yoke of kindness. Who could resist this? It's like telling a drowning man that he must put on the burden of a life preserver only to hear him shout back, sputtering, "No way! Not me! This is hard enough, drowning here in these stormy waters. The last thing I need is the added burden of a life preserver around my body!" That's what we all are like, confessing Christ with our lips but generally avoiding deep fellowship with him, out of a muted understanding of his heart.

His yoke is kind and his burden is light. That is, his yoke is a nonyoke, and his burden is a nonburden. What helium does to a balloon, Jesus's yoke does to his followers. We are buoyed along in life by his endless gentleness and supremely accessible lowliness. He doesn't simply meet us at our place of need; he lives in our place of need. He never tires of sweeping us into his tender embrace. It is his very heart. It is what gets him out of bed in the morning.

———

This is not how we intuitively think of Jesus Christ. Reflecting on this passage in Matthew 11, the old English pastor Thomas Goodwin helps us climb inside what Jesus is actually saying.

> Men are apt to have contrary conceits of Christ, but he tells them his disposition there, by preventing such hard thoughts of him, to allure them unto him the more. We are apt to think that he, being so holy, is therefore of a severe and sour disposition against sinners, and not able to bear them. "No," says he; "I am meek; gentleness is my nature and temper."[5]

We project onto Jesus our skewed instincts about how the world works. Human nature dictates that the wealthier a person, the more they tend to look down on the poor. The more beautiful a person, the more they are put off by the ugly. And without realizing what we are doing, we quietly assume that one so high and exalted has corresponding difficulty drawing near to the despicable and unclean. Sure, Jesus comes close to us, we agree—but he holds his nose. This risen Christ, after all, is the one whom "God has highly exalted,"

5 Thomas Goodwin, *The Heart of Christ* (Edinburgh: Banner of Truth, 2011), 63.

at whose name every knee will one day bow in submission (Phil. 2:9–11). This is the one whose eyes are "like a flame of fire" and whose voice is "like the roar of many waters" and who has "a sharp two-edged sword" coming out of his mouth and whose face is "like the sun shining in full strength" (Rev. 1:14–16); in other words, this is one so unspeakably brilliant that his resplendence cannot adequately be captured with words, so ineffably magnificent that all language dies away before his splendor.

This is the one whose deepest heart is, more than anything else, gentle and lowly.

Goodwin is saying that this high and holy Christ does not cringe at reaching out and touching dirty sinners and numbed sufferers. Such embrace is precisely what he loves to do. He cannot bear to hold back. We naturally think of Jesus touching us the way a little boy reaches out to touch a slug for the first time—face screwed up, cautiously extending an arm, giving a yelp of disgust upon contact, and instantly withdrawing. We picture the risen Christ approaching us with "a severe and sour disposition," as Goodwin says.

This is why we need a Bible. Our natural intuition can only give us a God like us. The God revealed in the Scripture deconstructs our intuitive predilections and startles us with one whose infinitude of perfections is matched by his infinitude of gentleness. Indeed, his perfections *include* his perfect gentleness.

It is who he is. It is his very heart. Jesus himself said so.

Come to me, all who labor and are heavy laden, and I will give you rest. Take my yoke upon you, and learn from me, for I am gentle and lowly in heart, and you will find rest for your souls. For my yoke is easy, and my burden is light.

2

His Heart in Action

And he had compassion on them.

MATTHEW 14:14

WHAT WE SEE JESUS CLAIM with his words in Matthew 11:29, we see him prove with his actions time and again in all four Gospels. What he is, he does. He cannot act any other way. His life proves his heart.

- When the leper says, "Lord, if you will, you can make me clean," Jesus immediately stretches out his hand and touches him, with the words, "I will; be clean" (Matt. 8:2–3). The word "will" in both the leper's request and in Jesus's answer is the Greek word for wish or desire. The leper was asking about Jesus's deepest desire. And Jesus revealed his deepest desire by healing him.

- When a group of men brings their paralyzed friend to Jesus, Jesus cannot even wait for them to ask him for what they want— "When Jesus *saw* their faith, he said to the paralytic, 'Take heart, my son; your sins are forgiven'" (Matt. 9:2). Before they could open their mouths to ask for help, Jesus couldn't stop himself—words of reassurance and calm tumbled out.

- Traveling from town to town, "he saw the crowds, [and] he had compassion for them, because they were harassed and helpless" (Matt. 9:36). So he teaches them, and he heals their diseases (Matt. 9:35). Simply seeing the helplessness of the throngs, pity ignites.

- This compassion comes in waves over and over again in Christ's ministry, driving him to heal the sick ("and he had compassion on them and healed their sick," Matt. 14:14), feed the hungry ("I have compassion on the crowd because they have been with me now three days and have nothing to eat," Matt. 15:32), teach the crowds ("and he had compassion on them . . . and he began to teach them many things," Mark 6:34), and wipe away the tears of the bereaved ("and he had compassion on her and said to her, 'Do not weep,'" Luke 7:13). The Greek word for "compassion" is the same in all these texts and refers most literally to the bowels or guts of a person—it's an ancient way of referring to what rises up from one's innermost core. This compassion reflects the deepest heart of Christ.

- Twice in the Gospels we are told that Jesus broke down and wept. And in neither case is it sorrow for himself or his own pains. In both cases it is sorrow over another—in one case, Jerusalem (Luke 19:41), and in the other, his deceased friend, Lazarus (John 11:35). What was his deepest anguish? The anguish of others. What drew his heart out to the point of tears? The tears of others.

- Time and again it is the morally disgusting, the socially reviled, the inexcusable and undeserving, who do not simply receive Christ's mercy but *to whom Christ most naturally gravitates.* He is, by his enemies' testimony, the "friend of sinners" (Luke 7:34).

When we take the Gospels as a whole and consider the composite picture given to us of who Jesus is, what stands out most strongly?

Yes, he is the fulfillment of the Old Testament hopes and longings (Matt. 5:17). Yes, he is one whose holiness causes even his friends to fall down in fear, aware of their sinfulness (Luke 5:8). Yes, he is a mighty teacher, one whose authority outstripped even that of the religious PhDs of the day (Mark 1:22). To diminish any of these is to step outside of vital historic orthodoxy. But the dominant note left ringing in our ears after reading the Gospels, the most vivid and arresting element of the portrait, is the way the Holy Son of God moves toward, touches, heals, embraces, and forgives those who least deserve it yet truly desire it.

The Puritan Richard Sibbes put it this way: "When [Christ] saw the people in misery, his bowels yearned within him; the works of grace and mercy in Christ, they come from his bowels first." That is, "whatsoever Christ did . . . he did it out of love, and grace, and mercy"—but then Sibbes goes one step deeper—"he did it inwardly from his very bowels."[1] The Jesus given to us in the Gospels is not simply one who loves, but one who is love; merciful affections stream from his innermost heart as rays from the sun.

---

1   Richard Sibbes, *The Church's Riches by Christ's Poverty,* in *The Works of Richard Sibbes,* ed. A. B. Grosart, 7 vols. (Edinburgh: Banner of Truth, 1983), 4:523.

But what about the harsher side of Jesus?

J. I. Packer once wrote that "a half-truth masquerading as the whole truth becomes a complete untruth."[2] This is an especially sensitive point when we are talking about the Bible's revelation of Christ. The heresies of church history are not universally upside-down depictions of Jesus but simply lopsided ones. The Christological controversies of the early centuries affirmed all basic Christian doctrine except one vital element—sometimes the true humanity of Christ, sometimes his true deity. Are we in danger, in talking of the heart of Christ, of neglecting his wrath? Extracting one side of Christ to the neglect of the other?

Perhaps for many of us the danger is subtler than outright heresy. We may be fully orthodox in our theology but drawn, for any number of reasons, to one side of Jesus more than another. Some of us may have been raised in a rules-heavy environment that suffocated us with an endless sense of not measuring up. We are drawn especially to the grace and mercy of Christ. Others of us may have grown up in a chaotic free-for-all, and the structure and order of a morally circumscribed life flowing from the commands of Christ may be especially attractive. Others of us have been deeply mistreated by those who should have been our protectors in life, and we long for the justice and retribution of heaven and hell to make right all wrongs.

As we zero in on the affectionate heart of Christ, how do we ensure that we are growing in a healthy understanding of the whole counsel of God and a comprehensive and therefore proportionate vision of who Christ is?

2   J. I. Packer, *A Quest for Godliness: The Puritan Vision of the Christian Life* (Wheaton, IL: Crossway, 1990), 126.

Three comments are needed here. First, the wrath of Christ and the mercy of Christ are not at odds with one another, like a see-saw, one diminishing to the degree that the other is held up. Rather, the two rise and fall together. The more robust one's felt understanding of the just wrath of Christ against all that is evil both around us and within us, the more robust our felt understanding of his mercy.

Second, in speaking specifically of the heart of Christ (and the heart of God in the Old Testament), we are not really on the wrath-mercy spectrum anyway. His heart is *his heart*. When we speak of Christ's heart, we are not so much speaking of one attribute alongside others. We are asking who he most deeply is. What pours out of him most naturally?

Third, we are simply seeking to follow the biblical witness in speaking of Christ's heart of affection toward sinners and sufferers. In other words, if there appears to be some sense of disproportion in the Bible's portrait of Christ, then let us be accordingly disproportionate. Better to be biblical than artificially "balanced."

Throughout the rest of our study we will return to the question of how to square the very heart of Christ with actions of his or biblical statements that may seem to sit awkwardly with it. But the above three points should be borne in mind throughout. In short: *it is impossible for the affectionate heart of Christ to be overcelebrated, made too much of, exaggerated.* It cannot be plumbed. But it is easily neglected, forgotten. We draw too little strength from it. We are not leaving behind the harsher side to Jesus as we speak of his very heart. Our sole aim is to follow the Bible's own testimony as we tunnel in to who Jesus most surprisingly is.

And if the actions of Jesus are reflective of who he most deeply is, we cannot avoid the conclusion that it is the very fallenness which he came to undo that is most irresistibly attractive to him.

———

This is deeper than saying Jesus is loving or merciful or gracious. The cumulative testimony of the four Gospels is that when Jesus Christ sees the fallenness of the world all about him, his deepest impulse, his most natural instinct, is to move toward that sin and suffering, not away from it.

One way to see this is against the backdrop of the Old Testament category of clean and unclean. In biblical terms these categories generally refer not to physical hygiene but to moral purity. The two cannot be completely disentangled, but moral or ethical cleanness is the primary meaning. This is evident in that the solution for uncleanness was not taking a bath but offering a sacrifice (Lev. 5:6). The problem was not dirt but guilt (Lev. 5:3). The Old Testament Jews, therefore, operated under a sophisticated system of degrees of uncleanness and various offerings and rituals to become morally clean once more. One particularly striking part of this system is that when an unclean person comes into contact with a clean person, that clean person then becomes unclean. Moral dirtiness is contagious.

Consider Jesus. In Levitical categories, he is the cleanest person to ever walk the face of the earth. He was the Clean One. Whatever horrors cause us to cringe—we who are naturally unclean and fallen—would cause Jesus to cringe all the more. We cannot fathom the sheer purity, holiness, cleanness, of his mind and heart. The simplicity, the innocence, the loveliness.

And what did he do when he saw the unclean? What was his first impulse when he came across prostitutes and lepers? He moved toward them. Pity flooded his heart, the longing of true compassion. He spent time with them. He touched them. We all can testify to the humaneness of touch. A warm hug does something warm words of greeting alone cannot. But there is something deeper in Christ's touch of compassion. He was reversing the Jewish system. When Jesus, the Clean One, touched an unclean sinner, Christ did not become unclean. The sinner became clean.

Jesus Christ's earthly ministry was one of giving back to undeserving sinners their humanity. We tend to think of the miracles of the Gospels as interruptions in the natural order. Yet German theologian Jürgen Moltmann points out that miracles are not an interruption of the natural order but the restoration of the natural order. We are so used to a fallen world that sickness, disease, pain, and death seem natural. In fact, *they* are the interruption.

> When Jesus expels demons and heals the sick, he is driving out of creation the powers of destruction, and is healing and restoring created beings who are hurt and sick. The lordship of God to which the healings witness, restores creation to health. Jesus' healings are not supernatural miracles in a natural world. They are the only truly "natural" thing in a world that is unnatural, demonized and wounded.[3]

3 Jürgen Moltmann, *The Way of Jesus Christ: Christology in Messianic Dimensions*, trans. M. Kohl (Minneapolis: Fortress, 1993), 98. Similarly Graeme Goldsworthy, *The Son of God and the New Creation*, Short Studies in Biblical Theology (Wheaton, IL: Crossway, 2015), 43.

Jesus walked the earth rehumanizing the dehumanized and cleansing the unclean. Why? Because his heart refused to let him sleep in. Sadness confronted him in every town. So wherever he went, whenever he was confronted with pain and longing, he spread the good contagion of his cleansing mercy. Thomas Goodwin said, "Christ is love covered over in flesh."[4] Picture it. Pull back the flesh on the Stepford Wives or the Terminator and you find machine; pull back the flesh on Christ and you find love.

If compassion clothed itself in a human body and went walking around this earth, what would it look like? We don't have to wonder.

———

But that was when he lived on earth. What about today?

Here we remember that the testimony of the New Testament is that "Jesus Christ is the same yesterday and today and forever" (Heb. 13:8). The same Christ who wept at the tomb of Lazarus weeps with us in our lonely despair. The same one who reached out and touched lepers puts his arm around us today when we feel misunderstood and sidelined. The Jesus who reached out and cleansed messy sinners reaches into our souls and answers our half-hearted plea for mercy with the mighty invincible cleansing of one who cannot bear to do otherwise.

In other words, Christ's heart is not far off despite his presence now in heaven, for he does all this by his own Spirit. We will give focused attention to the relationship between Christ's heart and the Holy Spirit in chapter 13. For now we simply note that through the Spirit, Christ himself not only touches us but lives within us.

4   Thomas Goodwin, *The Heart of Christ* (Edinburgh: Banner of Truth, 2011), 61.

The New Testament teaches that we are united to Christ, a union so intimate that whatever our own body parts do, Christ's body can be said to do (1 Cor. 6:15–16). *Jesus Christ is closer to you today than he was to the sinners and sufferers he spoke with and touched in his earthly ministry.* Through his Spirit, Christ's own heart envelops his people with an embrace nearer and tighter than any physical embrace could ever achieve. His actions on earth in a body reflected his heart; the same heart now acts in the same ways toward us, for *we* are now his body.

3

The Happiness of Christ

For the joy that was set before him . . .
HEBREWS 12:2

THOMAS GOODWIN WROTE that Christ's "own joy, comfort, happiness, and glory are increased and enlarged by . . ."

Now how would you finish that sentence?

There are various biblical ways to answer, and we should beware a one-dimensional portrait of Christ that elevates one to the neglect of others. It would be true to say that Jesus rejoices when his disciples forsake all to follow him (Mark 10:21–23). It would be valid to see Christ rejoicing when believers' faithfulness in a little prepares them to be faithful over much (Matt. 25:21, 23). We can affirm that he rejoices in the way his Father reveals divine truths to the childlike rather than the intellectually impressive (Luke 10:21).

But there is an equally biblical truth that is more easily sidelined in our thoughts of Christ. Christians intuitively know that it pleases Christ when we listen to him and obey him. But what if his very heart and joy is engaged in a new way in our foibles and failures?

Goodwin completes his sentence like this: Christ's "own joy, comfort, happiness, and glory are increased and enlarged by his showing grace and mercy, in pardoning, relieving, and comforting his members here on earth."[1]

———

A compassionate doctor has traveled deep into the jungle to provide medical care to a primitive tribe afflicted with a contagious disease. He has had his medical equipment flown in. He has correctly diagnosed the problem, and the antibiotics are prepared and available. He is independently wealthy and has no need of any kind of financial compensation. But as he seeks to provide care, the afflicted refuse. They want to take care of themselves. They want to heal on their own terms. Finally, a few brave young men step forward to receive the care being freely provided.

What does the doctor feel?

Joy.

His joy increases to the degree that the sick come to him for help and healing. It's the whole reason he came.

How much more if the diseased are not strangers but his own family?

So with us, and so with Christ. He does not get flustered and frustrated when we come to him for fresh forgiveness, for renewed

———

1   Thomas Goodwin, *The Heart of Christ* (Edinburgh: Banner of Truth, 2011), 107. Similarly Sibbes: "We cannot please Christ better than in showing ourselves welcome, by cheerful taking part of his rich provision. It is an honor to his bounty to fall to." Richard Sibbes, *Bowels Opened, Or, A Discovery of the Near and Dear Love, Union, and Communion Between Christ and the Church*, in *The Works of Richard Sibbes*, ed. A. B. Grosart, 7 vols. (repr., Edinburgh: Banner of Truth, 1983), 2:34.

pardon, with distress and need and emptiness. That's the whole point. It's what he came to heal. He went down into the horror of death and plunged out through the other side in order to provide a limitless supply of mercy and grace to his people.

But there's a deeper point Goodwin is making here. Jesus doesn't want us to draw on his grace and mercy only because it vindicates his atoning work. He wants us to draw on his grace and mercy because it is who he is. He drew near to us in the incarnation so that his joy and ours could rise and fall together—his in giving mercy, ours in receiving it. Goodwin even goes on to argue that *Christ gets more joy and comfort than we do* when we come to him for help and mercy. In the same way that a loving husband gets more relief and comfort in his wife's healing than in his own, Christ "brings in to himself more comfort . . . than it procures to them" when he sees our sins being placed under his own blood.[2]

Reflecting on Christ as our heavenly mediator—that is, the one who clears away any reason for us to be unable to enjoy friendship with God—he writes:

> [The] glory and happiness of Christ [are] enlarged and increased still, as his members come to have the purchase of his death more and more laid forth upon them; so as when their sins are pardoned, their hearts more sanctified, and their spirits comforted, then comes he to see the fruit of his labor, and is comforted thereby, for he is the more glorified by it, yea, he is much more pleased and rejoiced in this than themselves can be. And this keeps

up in his heart his care and love unto his children here below, to water and refresh them every moment.[3]

Translation: When you come to Christ for mercy and love and help in your anguish and perplexity and sinfulness, you are going with the flow of his own deepest wishes, not against them.

We tend to think that when we approach Jesus for help in our need and mercy amid our sins, we somehow detract from him, lessen him, impoverish him. Goodwin argues otherwise. Jesus surprises us in "exercising acts of grace, and from his continual doing good unto and for his members . . . from his filling them with all mercy, grace, comfort, and felicity, himself becoming yet more full, by filling them."[4] As truly God, Christ cannot become any more full; he shares in his Father's immortal, eternal, unchangeable fullness. Yet as truly man, Christ's heart is not drained by our coming to him; his heart is filled up all the more by our coming to him.

To put it the other way around: when we hold back, lurking in the shadows, fearful and failing, we miss out not only on our own increased comfort but on Christ's increased comfort. He lives for this. This is what he loves to do. His joy and ours rise and fall together.

---

3 Goodwin, *Heart of Christ*, 111–12.
4 Goodwin, *Heart of Christ*, 111. *Felicity* is an older term for happiness. As another older pastor movingly put it: "If you meet that poor wretch that thrust the spear into my side, tell him there is another way, a better way, of coming at my heart, if he will repent, and look upon whom he has pierced and will mourn. I will cherish him in that very bosom he has wounded; he shall find the blood he shed an ample atonement for the sin of shedding it. And tell him from me, he will put me to more pain and displeasure by refusing this offer of my blood, than when he drew it forth." Benjamin Grosvenor, "Grace to the Chief of Sinners," in *A Series of Tracts on the Doctrines, Order, and Polity of the Presbyterian Church in the United States of America*, vol. 3 (Philadelphia: Presbyterian Board of Publication, 1845), 42–43. I am grateful to Drew Hunter for drawing my attention to this reference.

But is this biblical?

Consider Hebrews 12. There Jesus is called "the founder and perfecter of our faith, who for the joy that was set before him endured the cross, despising the shame, and is seated at the right hand of the throne of God" (Heb. 12:2).

"For the joy." What joy? What was waiting for Jesus on the other side of the cross?

The joy of seeing his people forgiven.

Remember the whole point of Hebrews—Jesus is the high priest to end all high priests, who has made the final atoning sacrifice to completely cover the sins of his people so that they are provided for "to the uttermost" (7:25). And remember what the writer means when he speaks of Jesus sitting down at God's right hand, at the end of Hebrews 12:2. Elsewhere the writer to the Hebrews is explicit about what this signifies:

> After making purification for sins, he *sat down at the right hand* of the Majesty on high. (1:3)

> Now the point in what we are saying is this: we have such a high priest, one who is *seated at the right hand* of the throne of the Majesty in heaven. (8:1)

> But when Christ had offered for all time a single sacrifice for sins, he *sat down at the right hand* of God. (10:12)

In all these texts, Jesus's seating at God's right hand is associated with his priestly atoning work. The priest was the bridge between God and humanity. He reconnected heaven and earth. Jesus did this supremely through his climactic and final sacrifice of himself, purifying his people once and for all, cleansing them of their sins. It was the joyous anticipation of seeing his people made invincibly clean that sent him through his arrest, death, burial, and resurrection. When we today partake of that atoning work, coming to Christ for forgiveness, communing with him despite our sinfulness, we are laying hold of Christ's own deepest longing and joy.

This connects with other texts in the New Testament, such as the joy in heaven over a sinner repenting (Luke 15:7) or Christ's longing that his own joy would overlap with his disciples' joy as they abide in his love (John 15:11; 17:13). He wants us to draw strength from his love, but the only ones qualified to do that are sinners in need of undeserved love. And he doesn't just want us to be forgiven. He wants *us*. How does Jesus speak of his own deepest desires? Like this: "Father, I desire that they also, whom you have given me, may be with me" (John 17:24).

———

Our unbelieving hearts tread cautiously here. Is it not presumptuous audacity to draw on the mercy of Christ in an unfiltered way? Shouldn't we be measured and reasonable, careful not to pull too much on him?

Would a father with a suffocating child want his child to draw on the oxygen tank in a measured, reasonable way?

Our trouble is that we do not take the Scripture seriously when it speaks of us as Christ's body. Christ is the head; we are his own body parts. How does a head feel about his own flesh? The apostle Paul tells us: "He nourishes and cherishes it" (Eph. 5:29). And then Paul makes the explicit connection to Christ: "just as Christ does the church, because we are members of his body" (5:29–30). How do we care for a wounded body part? We nurse it, bandage it, protect it, give it time to heal. For that body part isn't just a close friend; it is part of us. So with Christ and believers. We are part of him. This is why the risen Christ asks a persecutor of his *people*, "Why are you persecuting *me*?" (Acts 9:4).

Jesus Christ is comforted when you draw from the riches of his atoning work, because his own body is getting healed.

4

Able to Sympathize

*We do not have a high priest who is unable
to sympathize with our weaknesses.*

HEBREWS 4:15

THE WAY THE PURITANS WOULD write books is to take a single Bible verse, wring it dry for all the heart-affecting theology they could find, and, two or three hundred pages later, send their findings to a publisher. Thomas Goodwin's *The Heart of Christ* is no different. And the verse being wrung dry is Hebrews 4:15:

> For we do not have a high priest who is unable to sympathize with our weaknesses, but one who in every respect has been tempted as we are, yet without sin.

Goodwin's burden is to convince disheartened believers that even though Christ is now in heaven, he is just as open and tender in his embrace of sinners and sufferers as ever he was on earth. The original title page of the book from its 1651 publication reflects this; note especially the prominent juxtaposition between "Christ in heaven" and "sinners on earth":

THE

HEART

OF

CHRIST IN HEAVEN

Towards

SINNERS on Earth.

OR,

A TREATISE

DEMONSTRATING

The gracious Disposition and tender
Affection of *Christ* in his Humane Nature now in
Glory, unto his Members under all sorts of
Infirmities, either of *Sin* or *Misery*

The closing lines clarify that by Christ's *heart*, he means Christ's "gracious disposition and tender affection." Goodwin wants to surprise readers with the biblical evidence that the risen Lord alive and well in heaven today is not somehow less approachable and less compassionate than he was when he walked the earth.

After an introductory section, Goodwin explains why he has picked Hebrews 4:15 to explore this point:

I have chosen this text, as that which above any other speaks his heart most, and sets out the frame and workings of it towards sinners; and that so sensibly that it does, as it were, take our hands, and lay them upon Christ's breast, and let us feel how his heart beats and his affections yearn toward us, even now he is in glory—the very scope of these words being manifestly to encourage believers against all that may discourage them, from the consideration of Christ's heart toward them now in heaven.[1]

What would it be like for a friend to take our two hands and place them on the chest of the risen Lord Jesus Christ so that, like a stethoscope letting us hear the vigorous strength of a beating heart physically, our hands let us feel the vigorous strength of Christ's deepest affections and longings? Goodwin is saying: We don't have to wonder. Hebrews 4:15 is that friend.

———

The broader context of Hebrews 4:15 is worth keeping before us. Stepping back slightly, the fuller passage goes like this:

> Since then we have a great high priest who has passed through the heavens, Jesus, the Son of God, let us hold fast our confession. *For we do not have a high priest who is unable to sympathize with our weaknesses, but one who in every respect has been tempted as we are, yet without sin.* Let us then with confidence draw near to the throne of grace, that we may receive mercy and find grace to help in time of need. (4:14–16)

Verses 14 and 16 each contain an exhortation: fidelity in doctrine about God ("Let us hold fast our confession," v. 14) and confidence in communion with God ("Let us then with confidence draw near,"

---

1   Thomas Goodwin, *The Heart of Christ* (Edinburgh: Banner of Truth, 2011), 48.

v. 16). The "For" that begins verse 15 (the italicized verse above) signifies that verse 15 grounds verse 14. And the "then" toward the beginning of verse 16 signifies that verse 15 grounds verse 16 too. In other words, verse 15 is the anchor of the passage, the surrounding verses drawing out its implications.

The burden of this anchor verse is Jesus Christ's sheer *solidarity* with his people. All our natural intuitions tell us that Jesus is with us, on our side, present and helping, when life is going well. This text says the opposite. It is in "our weaknesses" that Jesus sympathizes with us. The word for "sympathize" here is a compound word formed from the prefix meaning "with" (like our English prefix *co-*) joined with the verb *to suffer*. "Sympathize" here is not cool and detached pity. It is a depth of felt solidarity such as is echoed in our own lives most closely only as parents to children. Indeed, it is deeper even than that. In our pain, Jesus is pained; in our suffering, he feels the suffering as his own even though it isn't—not that his invincible divinity is threatened, but in the sense that his heart is feelingly drawn into our distress. His human nature engages our troubles comprehensively.[2] His is a love that cannot be held back when he sees his people in pain.

The writer to the Hebrews is taking us by the hand and leading us deep into the heart of Christ, showing us the unrestrained *withness* of Jesus regarding his people. Back in chapter 2 the writer to the Hebrews had said that Jesus was "made like his brothers in every

---

2   On his human (as distinct from divine) nature as specifically what is engaged in Christ's felt solidarity with his people in their sufferings, see esp. John Owen, *An Exposition of the Epistle to the Hebrews*, in *The Works of John Owen*, vol. 25, ed. W. H. Goold (repr., Edinburgh: Banner of Truth, 1965), 416–28.

respect" and that "he himself suffered when tempted" (using the same Greek word for tempted/tested that occurs in 4:15).

The real scandal of Hebrews 4:15, though, is what we are told about why Jesus is so close and with his people in their pain. He has been "tempted" (or "tested," as the word can also denote) "as we are"—not only that, but "in every respect" as we are. The reason that Jesus is in such close solidarity with us is that the difficult path we are on is not unique to us. He has journeyed on it himself. It is not only that Jesus can relieve us from our troubles, like a doctor prescribing medicine; it is also that, before any relief comes, he is with us in our troubles, like a doctor who has endured the same disease.

Jesus is not Zeus. He was a sinless man, not a sinless Superman. He woke up with bed head. He had pimples at thirteen. He never would have appeared on the cover of *Men's Health* (he had "no beauty that we should desire him," Isa. 53:2). He came as a normal man to normal men. He knows what it is to be thirsty, hungry, despised, rejected, scorned, shamed, embarrassed, abandoned, misunderstood, falsely accused, suffocated, tortured, and killed. He knows what it is to be lonely. His friends abandoned him when he needed them most; had he lived today, every last Twitter follower and Facebook friend would have un-friended him when he turned thirty-three—he who will never un-friend us.

The key to understanding the significance of Hebrews 4:15 is to push equally hard on the two phrases "in every respect" *and* "yet without sin." All our weakness—indeed, all of our life—is tainted with sin. If sin were the color blue, we do not occasionally say or do something blue; all that we say, do, and think has some taint of blue. Not so Jesus. He had no sin. He was "holy, innocent, unstained, separated from sinners" (Heb. 7:26–27). But we must ponder the phrase "in every respect" in a way that maintains Jesus's sinlessness without diluting what that phrase means. That enticing temptation, that sore trial, that bewildering perplexity—he has been there. Indeed, his utter purity suggests that he has felt these pains more acutely than we sinners ever could.

———

Consider your own life.

When the relationship goes sour, when the feelings of futility come flooding in, when it feels like life is passing us by, when it seems that our one shot at significance has slipped through our fingers, when we can't sort out our emotions, when the longtime friend lets us down, when a family member betrays us, when we feel deeply misunderstood, when we are laughed at by the impressive—in short, when the fallenness of the world closes in on us and makes us want to throw in the towel—there, right there, we have a Friend who knows exactly what such testing feels like, and sits close to us, embraces us. With us. Solidarity.

Our tendency is to feel intuitively that the more difficult life gets, the more alone we are. As we sink further into pain, we sink further into felt isolation. The Bible corrects us. Our pain never outstrips what he himself shares in. We are never alone. That sorrow that feels so isolating, so unique, was endured by him in the past and is now shouldered by him in the present.

As verse 14 tells us, Jesus has now gone up into heaven. But that does not mean he is distant or aloof from our pains. Verse 15, Goodwin says, "lets us understand how feelingly and sensibly affected the heart of Christ is to sinners under all . . . their infirmities."[3] Our difficulties draw out a depth of feeling in Christ beyond what we know.

But what about our sins? Should we be discouraged that Jesus can't be in solidarity with us in that most piercing of pains, the guilt and shame of our sin? No, for two reasons.

One is that Jesus's sinlessness means that he knows temptation better than we ourselves do. C. S. Lewis made this point by speaking of a man walking against the wind. Once the wind of temptation gets strong enough, the man lies down, giving in—and thus not knowing what it would have been like ten minutes later. Jesus never lay down; he endured all our temptations and testings without ever giving in. He therefore knows the strength of temptation better than any of us. Only he truly knows the cost.[4]

The second reason is that our only hope is that the one who shares in all our pain shares in it as the pure and holy one. Our sinless high priest is not one who needs rescue but who provides it. This is why we can go to him to "receive mercy and find grace" (4:16). He himself is not trapped in the hole of sin with us; he alone can pull us out. His sinlessness is our salvation. But here we are beginning to move over into the work of Christ. The burden of Hebrews 4:15, and of Thomas Goodwin's book on it, is the heart of Christ. Yes, verse 16 speaks of "the throne of grace." But verse 15 is opening up to us the heart of grace. Not only can he alone pull us out of the hole of sin; he alone desires to climb in and bear our burdens. Jesus is able to sympathize. He "co-suffers" with us. As Goodwin's contemporary John Owen put it, Christ "is inclined

3 Goodwin, *Heart of Christ*, 50.
4 C. S. Lewis, *Mere Christianity* (New York: Touchstone, 1996), 126.

from his own heart and affections to give . . . us help and relief . . . and he is inwardly moved during our sufferings and trials with a sense and fellow-feeling of them."[5]

If you are in Christ, you have a Friend who, in your sorrow, will never lob down a pep talk from heaven. He cannot bear to hold himself at a distance. Nothing can hold him back. His heart is too bound up with yours.

5   John Owen, *An Exposition of the Epistle to the Hebrews*, in *The Works of John Owen*, vol. 21, ed. W. H. Goold (repr., Edinburgh: Banner of Truth, 1968), 422.

5

He Can Deal Gently

He can deal gently with the ignorant and wayward.
HEBREWS 5:2

IN ANCIENT ISRAEL THE KING represented God to the people, while the priest represented the people to God. The king provided authority over the people; the priest provided solidarity with the people. The book of Hebrews is in the Bible to tell us what it means for Jesus to be our priest, the true priest, the priest of whom every other is a shadow and to whom every other is a pointer.

The priests of Israel were themselves sinful. So they needed to offer sacrifices not only for the sins of the people but also for their own sins. Not only were the priests of Israel sinners by definition; they were clearly sinners by practice. Some priests of old were among the more heinous characters of the Old Testament—think Hophni and Phinehas, for example (1 Sam. 1–4). We today need a priest no less than ancient Israelites. We need someone to represent us to God. But the priests of old were at times so disappointing, so evil, so harsh.

51

But if our priest himself knew what our weakness felt like so that
he was in deepest sympathy with us, yet had never himself sinned,
and so his heart had never turned in on himself in self-pity or self-
absorption—that would be a priest truly able to deal gently with us.

———

Hebrews 5 continues the line of thought considered in our last
chapter, where we looked at the end of Hebrews 4. There we considered the way in which Christ's heart is drawn out to his people
in solidarity with them in their pain and distress. Now in Hebrews
5:2 we consider a further truth—the manner in which he handles
his people to whom he is drawn. We see the *what* of Christ's priestly
role in 4:15, the *how* in 5:2.

And what is the *how*?

Gently.

The Greek word underlying "deal gently" in 5:2 shares a common
root with "sympathize" in 4:15, and the original hearers and readers of
Hebrews would likely have picked up on this in a way that is missed in
English. We also find in both texts the repeated Greek verb *dunamai*,
even in the same verbal form (though one does not readily see that in
the divergent renderings of "able to" and "can"), as well as a repeated
mention of "weakness" (which we'll return to later in this chapter).
Let me give you the two phrases transliterated so that you can get
a sense of the parallel that the original hearers would have noticed:

> 4:15 *dunamenon sunpathesai tois* ("able to sympathize with
> the . . .")
> 5:2 *metriopathein dunamenon tois* ("He can deal gently with
> the . . .")

Along with the repeated word *dunamenon*, which means "one who is able to" or "one who has the capability to," note the common root to the key verb in each verse, which I've underlined. We noted in the previous chapter that *sunpathesai* means to "cosuffer" in the sense of feeling out of his full solidarity with us. While you can see the way this Greek word gives us our English word *sympathy*, the meaning is richer than *sympathy* tends to denote to our minds. Now in 5:2, as the writer continues to lay out how Jesus is our great high priest, we find the word *metriopathein*. This is the only use of this verb in the New Testament. It means exactly what is given in the text: to deal gently. The prefix *metrio-* has the sense of restraint or moderation, and the root *patheo* refers to passion or suffering. The idea here in 5:2 is that Jesus does not throw his hands up in the air when he engages sinners. He is calm, tender, soothing, restrained. He deals with us gently.

———

With whom does he "deal gently"? Those of reasonable and moderate failure, surely—reserving a harsher response for the bigger sinners?

A careful reading of the text does not allow us to conclude this. "He can deal gently with the ignorant and wayward." The ignorant and wayward are not two kinds of milder sinners, cordoned off from the major sinners. No, this is the writer's way of including everyone. In the Old Testament—and remember how richly and pervasively built out of the Old Testament this letter to the Hebrews is—we find that there were basically two kinds of sins: unwillful and willful, or accidental and deliberate, or as Numbers 15 puts it, unintentional and "with a high hand" (Num. 15:27–31). This is almost certainly what the writer to the Hebrews has in mind, with "ignorant" refer-ring to accidental sins and "wayward" referring to deliberate sins.

In other words, when Hebrews 5:2 says that Jesus "can deal gently with the ignorant and the wayward," the point is that Jesus deals gently and only gently with all sinners who come to him, irrespective of their particular offense and just how heinous it is.[1] What elicits tenderness from Jesus is not the severity of the sin but whether the sinner comes to him. Whatever our offense, he deals gently with us. If we never come to him, we will experience a judgment so fierce it will be like a double-edged sword coming out of his mouth at us (Rev. 1:16; 2:12; 19:15, 21). If we do come to him, as fierce as his lion-like judgment would have been against us, so deep will be his lamb-like tenderness for us (cf. Rev. 5:5–6; Isa. 40:10–11). We will be enveloped in one or the other. To no one will Jesus be neutral.

Consider what all this means. When we sin, we are encouraged to bring our mess to Jesus because he will know just how to receive us. He doesn't handle us roughly. He doesn't scowl and scold. He doesn't lash out, the way many of our parents did. And all this restraint on his part is not because he has a diluted view of our sinfulness. He knows our sinfulness far more deeply than we do. Indeed, we are aware of just the tip of the iceberg of our depravity, even in our most searching moments of self-knowledge. His restraint simply flows from his tender heart for his people. Hebrews is not just telling us that instead of scolding us, Jesus loves us. It's telling us the kind of

---

1 Owen argues this point and expresses it with particular elegance: John Owen, *An Exposi-tion of the Epistle to the Hebrews*, in *The Works of John Owen*, vol. 21, ed. W. H. Goold (repr., Edinburgh: Banner of Truth, 1968), 457–61.

love he has: rather than dispensing grace to us from on high, he gets down with us, he puts his arm around us, he deals with us in the way that is just what we need. He deals gently with us.

Perhaps the most significant commentary yet written on the letter to the Hebrews was the work of John Owen. Of the twenty-three volumes that presently make up Owen's collected works, seven of these are a verse-by-verse walk-through of Hebrews.[2] This took him almost twenty years to complete, the first volume being published in 1668 and the last one in 1684. What does this great expositor of Hebrews say about what Hebrews 5:2 is trying to tell us? Owen writes that when we are told that the high priest "can deal gently with the ignorant and the wayward," this means that he can

> no more cast off poor sinners for their ignorance and wanderings than a nursing father should cast away a sucking child for its crying. . . . Thus ought it to be with a high priest, and thus is it with Jesus Christ. He is able, with all meekness and gentleness, with patience and moderation, to bear with the infirmities, sins, and provocations of his people, even as a nurse or a nursing father bears with the weakness . . . of a poor infant.[3]

Jesus can no more bring himself to stiff-arm you than the loving father of a crying newborn can bring himself to stiff-arm his dear child. Jesus's heart is drawn out to you. Nothing can chain his affections to heaven; his heart is too swollen with endearing love.

2 I refer to the edition published by Banner of Truth (Edinburgh, 1968). A new critical edition of Owen's works is being prepared by Crossway that is projected to spread over thirty volumes.
3 Owen, *Works*, 21:455–56.

More than this, Christ's "meekness and gentleness," his "patience and moderation," is not peripheral or accidental to who Christ is, as if his truest delights lie elsewhere. This very care, this gentle dealing with all kinds of sinners, is what is most natural to him. Owen goes on to say that Christ "does not, in his dealings with us, more properly or more fully set out any property of his nature than he does his compassion, long-suffering, and forbearance."[4] In other words, when Jesus "deals gently" with us, he is doing what is most fitting and natural to him.

Indeed, given the depths of our sinfulness, the fact that Jesus has not yet cast us off proves that his deepest impulse and delight is patient gentleness. Owen says that this gentle dealing by the high priest "as applied to Jesus Christ, is a matter of the highest encouragement and consolation unto believers. Were there not an absolute sufficiency of this disposition in him, and that as unto all occurrences, he must needs cast us all off in displeasure."[5] That's Owen's old-fashioned, clunky way of saying: Our sinfulness runs so deep that a tepid measure of gentleness from Jesus would not be enough; but as deep our sinfulness runs, ever deeper runs his gentleness.

———

But why? Why does Christ deal gently with us?

The text tells us: "since he himself is beset with weakness."

Most immediately, this refers to the high priesthood generally. This is clear from the next verse, which speaks of the high priest needing to offer sacrifice for his own sins (5:3), which Jesus did not

4 Owen, *Works*, 21:462.
5 Owen, *Works*, 21:454.

need to do (7:27). But remember what we saw a few verses earlier in 4:15—Jesus himself, while "without sin," is able to "sympathize with our *weaknesses*" (same Greek word as in 5:2) as "one who in every respect has been tempted as we are." Jesus had zero sin. But he did experience everything else that it means to live as a real human being in this fallen world: the weakness of suffering, temptation, and every other kind of human limitation (see also 2:14–18). The various high priests through Israel's history were sinfully weak; Jesus the high priest was sinlessly weak (cf. 2 Cor. 13:5).

Contrary to what we expect to be the case, therefore, the deeper into weakness and suffering and testing we go, the deeper Christ's solidarity with us. As we go down into pain and anguish, we are descending ever deeper *into* Christ's very heart, not away from it.

Look to Christ. He deals gently with you. It's the only way he knows how to be. He is the high priest to end all high priests. As long as you fix your attention on your sin, you will fail to see how you can be safe. But as long as you look to this high priest, you will fail to see how you can be in danger. Looking inside ourselves, we can anticipate only harshness from heaven. Looking out to Christ, we can anticipate only gentleness.

6

I Will Never Cast Out

Whoever comes to me I will never cast out.
JOHN 6:37

EVERYTHING THAT THOMAS GOODWIN and John Owen were—erudite, well-educated, analytical, at home in the world's best universities—John Bunyan wasn't. Bunyan was poor and uneducated. By the world's standards, everything was against Bunyan's making a lasting impact on human history. But this is just how the Lord delights to work—taking the sidelined and the overlooked and giving them quietly pivotal roles in the unfolding of redemptive history. And Bunyan, though much earthier in writing style, shared Goodwin's ability to open up the heart of Christ to his readers.

Bunyan is most famous for *The Pilgrim's Progress*, which is, besides the Bible, history's best-selling book. But he also authored fifty-seven other books. One of the loveliest is *Come and Welcome to Jesus Christ*, written in 1678. The warmth of the title is representative of the entire treatise. In typical Puritan style, Bunyan took a single verse and wrote a whole book on it, reflecting on it at length. That verse, for *Come and Welcome to Jesus Christ*, was John 6:37. In the course of pronouncing himself the bread of life given to the spiritually hungry (John 6:32–40), Jesus declares:

> All that the Father gives me will come to me, and whoever comes to me I will never cast out.

It was one of Bunyan's favorite verses, as evident from how often he cites it throughout his writings. But in this particular book he takes the text and zeroes in on it, looking at it from every angle, wringing it dry.

There is a mountain of consoling theology packed into this single verse. Consider what Jesus says:

- "All . . . ," not "most." Once the Father sets his loving gaze on a wandering sinner, that sinner's rescue is certain.

- ". . . the Father . . ." Our redemption is not a matter of a gracious Son trying to calm down an uncontrollably angry Father. The Father himself ordains our deliverance. He takes the loving initiative (note v. 38).

- ". . . gives . . . ," not "haggles over." It is the Father's deep delight to freely entrust recalcitrant rebels into the gracious care of his Son.

- ". . . will come . . ." God's saving purpose for a sinner is never thwarted. He is never frustrated. He never runs out of resources. If the Father calls us, we *will* come to Christ.

- ". . . and whoever comes . . ." Yet we are not robots. While the Father is clearly the sovereign overseer of our redemption, we are not dragged kicking and screaming into Christ against our will.

Divine grace is so radical that it reaches down and turns around our very desires. Our eyes are opened. Christ becomes beautiful. We come to him. And anyone—"whoever"—is welcome. Come and welcome to Jesus Christ.

- ". . . comes to me . . ." We do not come to a set of doctrines. We do not come to a church. We do not even come to the gospel. All these are vital. But most truly, we come to a person, to Christ himself.

———

Bunyan draws out all this and more. The book is worth reading in full.[1] But it is the final words of the verse that he dwells longest on, that meant most to him. At the center of his book he confronts our innate suspicions of Christ's deepest heart. Using his KJV rendering ("Him that cometh to me I will in no wise cast out"), Bunyan writes:

> They that are coming to Jesus Christ, are often times heartily afraid that Jesus Christ will not receive them.
>
> This observation is implied in the text. I gather it from the largeness and openness of the promise: "I will in no wise cast out." For had there not been a proneness in us to "fear casting out," Christ needed not to have waylaid our fear, as he does by this great and strange expression, "In no wise."
>
> There needed not, as I may say, such a promise to be invented by the wisdom of heaven, and worded at such a rate, as it were on

---

1 It exists as a stand-alone volume, published by Banner of Truth: *Come and Welcome to Jesus Christ* (Edinburgh: Banner of Truth, 2004); it can also be found in vol. 1 of *The Works of John Bunyan*, 3 vols., ed. George Offor (repr., Edinburgh: Banner of Truth, 1991), 240–99.

purpose to dash in pieces at one blow all the objections of coming sinners, if they were not prone to admit of such objections, to the discouraging of their own souls.

For this word, "in no wise," cuts the throat of all objections; and it was dropped by the Lord Jesus for that very end; and to help the faith that is mixed with unbelief. And it is, as it were, the sum of all promises; neither can any objection be made upon the unworthiness that you find in yourself, that this promise will not assoil.

But I am a great sinner, say you.
"I will in no wise cast out," says Christ.
But I am an old sinner, say you.
"I will in no wise cast out," says Christ.
But I am a hard-hearted sinner, say you.
"I will in no wise cast out," says Christ.
But I am a backsliding sinner, say you.
"I will in no wise cast out," says Christ.
But I have served Satan all my days, say you.
"I will in no wise cast out," says Christ.
But I have sinned against light, say you.
"I will in no wise cast out," says Christ.
But I have sinned against mercy, say you.
"I will in no wise cast out," says Christ.
But I have no good thing to bring with me, say you.
"I will in no wise cast out," says Christ.

This promise was provided to answer all objections, and does answer them.[2]

---

2   Bunyan, *Come and Welcome to Jesus Christ*, in *Works*, 1:279–80; language lightly updated.

We no longer use the expression "in no wise," but it was a seventeenth-century English way of capturing the emphatic negative of the Greek of John 6:37. The text literally reads, "the one coming to me I will not—*not*—cast out." Sometimes, as here, Greek uses two negatives piled on top of each other for literary forcefulness. "I will most certainly never, ever cast out." It is this emphatic negation that Christ will ever cast us out that Bunyan calls "this great and strange expression."

What is Bunyan after?

Jesus's statement in John 6:37, and the book *Come and Welcome to Jesus Christ*, and this quote at the center of that book, all exist to calm us with the *persevering* nature of the heart of Christ. We say, "But I . . ." He says, "I will never cast out."

Fallen, anxious sinners are limitless in their capacity to perceive reasons for Jesus to cast them out. We are factories of fresh resistances to Christ's love. Even when we run out of tangible reasons to be cast out, such as specific sins or failures, we tend to retain a vague sense that, given enough time, Jesus will finally grow tired of us and hold us at arm's length. Bunyan understands us. He knows we tend to deflect Christ's assurances.

"No, wait"—we say, cautiously approaching Jesus—"you don't understand. I've *really* messed up, in all kinds of ways."

I know, he responds.

"You know most of it, sure. Certainly more than what others see. But there's perversity down inside me that is hidden from everyone."

I know it all.

"Well—the thing is, it isn't just my past. It's my present too."

I understand.

"But I don't know if I can break free of this any time soon."

That's the only kind of person I'm here to help.

"The burden is heavy—and heavier all the time."

Then let me carry it.

"It's too much to bear."

Not for me.

"You don't get it. My offenses aren't directed toward others. They're against you."

Then I am the one most suited to forgive them.

"But the more of the ugliness in me you discover, the sooner you'll get fed up with me."

Whoever comes to me I will never cast out.

———

With mouth-stopping defiance Bunyan concludes his list of objections we raise to coming to Jesus. "This promise was provided to answer all objections, and does answer them." Case closed. We cannot present a reason for Christ to finally close off his heart to his own sheep. No such reason exists. Every human friend has a limit. If we offend enough, if a relationship gets damaged enough, if we betray enough times, we are cast out. The walls go up. With Christ, our sins and weaknesses are the very resumé items that qualify us to approach him. Nothing but coming to him is required—first at conversion and a thousand times thereafter until we are with him upon death.

Perhaps it isn't sins so much as sufferings that cause some of us to question the perseverance of the heart of Christ. As pain piles up, as numbness takes over, as the months go by, at some point the conclusion seems obvious: we have been cast out. Surely this is not what life would feel like for one who has been buried in the heart of a gentle and lowly Savior? But Jesus does not say that those with pain-free lives are never cast out. He says those who come to him are never cast out. It is not what life brings to us but to whom we belong that determines Christ's heart of love for us.

The only thing required to enjoy such love is to come to him. To ask him to take us in. He does not say, "Whoever comes to me with sufficient contrition," or "Whoever comes to me feeling bad enough for their sin," or "Whoever comes to me with redoubled efforts." He says, "Whoever comes to me I will never cast out."

Our strength of resolve is not part of the formula of retaining his good will. When my two-year-old Benjamin begins to wade into the gentle slope of the zero-entry swimming pool near our home, he instinctively grabs hold of my hand. He holds on tight as the water gradually gets deeper. But a two-year-old's grip is not very strong. Before long it is not he holding on to me but me holding on to him. Left to his own strength he will certainly slip out of my hand. But if I have determined that he will not fall out of my grasp, he is secure. He can't get away from me if he tried.

So with Christ. We cling to him, to be sure. But our grip is that of a two-year-old amid the stormy waves of life. His sure grasp never falters. Psalm 63:8 expresses the double-sided truth: "My soul clings to you; your right hand upholds me."

We are talking about something deeper than the doctrine of eternal security, or "once saved, always saved"—a glorious doctrine, a true doctrine—sometimes called the perseverance of the saints.

We have come, more deeply, to the doctrine of the perseverance of the heart of Christ. Yes, professing Christians can fall away, proving that they were never truly in Christ. Yes, once a sinner is united to Christ, there is nothing that can dis-unite them. But within the skeletal structure of these doctrines, what is the beating heart of God, made tangible in Christ? What is most deeply instinctive to him as our sins and sufferings pile up? What keeps him from growing cold? The answer is, his heart. The atoning work of the Son, decreed by the Father and applied by the Spirit, ensures that we are safe eternally. But a text such as John 6:37 reassures us that this is not only a matter of divine decree but divine desire. This is heaven's delight. Come to me, says Christ. I will embrace you into my deepest being and never let you go.

Have you considered what is true of you if you are in Christ? In order for you to fall short of loving embrace into the heart of Christ both now and into eternity, Christ himself would have to be pulled down out of heaven and put back in the grave. His death and resurrection make it just for Christ never to cast out his own, no matter how often they fall. But animating this work of Christ is the heart of Christ. He cannot bear to part with his own, even when they most deserve to be forsaken.

"But I . . ."

Raise your objections. None can threaten these invincible words: "Whoever comes to me I will never cast out."

For those united to him, the heart of Jesus is not a rental; it is your new permanent residence. You are not a tenant; you are a child. His heart is not a ticking time bomb; his heart is the green pastures and still waters of endless reassurances of his presence and comfort, whatever our present spiritual accomplishments. It is who he is.

7

What Our Sins Evoke

My heart recoils within me.
HOSEA 11:8

IT IS PROBABLY IMPOSSIBLE to conceive of the horror of hell and of the ferocity of retributive justice and righteous wrath that will sweep over those found on the last day to be out of Christ. Perhaps a word like *ferocity* here makes it sound as if God's wrath will be uncontrolled or blown out of proportion. But there is nothing uncontrolled or disproportionate in God.

The reason we feel as if divine wrath can easily be overstated is that we do not feel the true weight of sin. Martyn Lloyd-Jones, reflecting on this, said:

> You will never make yourself feel that you are a sinner, because there is a mechanism in you as a result of sin that will always be defending you against every accusation. We are all on very good terms with ourselves, and we can always put up a good case for ourselves. Even if we try to make ourselves feel that we

are sinners, we will never do it. There is only one way to know that we are sinners, and that is to have some dim, glimmering conception of God.[1]

In other words, we don't feel the weight of our sin because of: our sin. If we saw with deeper clarity just how insidious and pervasive and revolting sin is—and, as Lloyd-Jones suggests above, we can see this only as we see the beauty and holiness of God—we would know that human evil calls for an intensity of judgment of divine proportion. Even someone with such a profound sense of the loving heart of Christ as Thomas Goodwin has no trouble likewise asserting that if "his wrath against sin was the fire," then "all earthly bellows would . . . not have been able to make the furnace hot enough."[2]

And just as we can hardly fathom the divine ferocity awaiting those out of Christ, it is equally true that we can hardly fathom the divine tenderness already resting now on those in Christ. We might feel a little bashful or uncomfortable or even guilty in emphasizing God's tenderness as intensively as his wrath. But the Bible feels no such discomfort. Consider Romans 5:20: "Where sin increased, grace abounded all the more." The guilt and shame of those in Christ is ever outstripped by his abounding grace. When we feel as if our thoughts, words, and deeds are diminishing God's grace toward us, those sins and failures are in fact causing it to surge forward all the more.

1 Martyn Lloyd-Jones, *Seeking the Face of God: Nine Reflections on the Psalms* (Wheaton, IL: Crossway, 2005), 34.

2 Thomas Goodwin, *Of Gospel Holiness in the Heart and Life*, in *The Works of Thomas Goodwin*, 12 vols. (repr., Grand Rapids, MI: Reformation Heritage, 2006), 7:194.

But let's press into this inviolable principle in the economy of the gospel. We've been speaking of God's grace and the way it is drawn out always to match abundantly the need for it. But there is, purely speaking, no such "thing" as grace. That's Roman Catholic theology, in which grace is a kind of stockpiled treasure that can be accessed through various carefully controlled means. But the grace of God comes to us no more and no less than Jesus Christ comes to us. In the biblical gospel we are not given a thing; we are given a person.

Let's drill in even deeper. What are we given when we are given Christ? More acutely, if we can speak of grace as always being drawn out in our sin but as coming to us only in Christ himself, then we are confronted with a vital aspect of who Christ is—a biblical aspect that the Puritans loved to reflect on: *when we sin, the very heart of Christ is drawn out to us.*

———

This may cause some of us to cringe. If Christ is perfectly holy, must he not necessarily withdraw from sin?

Here we enter in to one of the profoundest mysteries of who God in Christ is. Not only are holiness and sinfulness mutually exclusive, but Christ, being perfectly holy, knows and feels the horror and weight of sin more deeply than any of us sinful ones could—just as the purer a man's heart, the more horrified he is at the thought of his neighbors being robbed or abused. Conversely, the more corrupt one's heart, the less one is affected by the evils all around.

Carry the analogy a little further. Just as the purer a heart, the more horrified at evil, so also the purer a heart, the more it is naturally drawn out to help and relieve and protect and comfort, whereas a corrupt heart sits still, indifferent. So with Christ. His holiness finds evil revolting, more revolting than any of us ever could feel. But it is that very holiness that also draws his heart out to help and relieve and protect and comfort. Again we must bear in mind the all-crucial distinction between those not in Christ and those in Christ. For those who do not belong to him, sins evoke holy wrath. How could a morally serious God respond otherwise? But to those who do belong to him, sins evoke holy longing, holy love, holy tenderness. In the key text on divine holiness (Isa. 6:1–8), that holiness (6:3) flows naturally and immediately into forgiveness and mercy (6:7).

Here's how Goodwin explains it as he brings to a close his book *The Heart of Christ* with a series of concluding applications. Reflecting on the "consolations and encouragements" that are ours in light of Christ himself feeling pain in our own sins and sufferings, he writes:

> There is comfort concerning such infirmities, in that your very sins move him to pity more than to anger. . . . For he suffers with us under our infirmities, and by infirmities are meant sins, as well as other miseries. . . . Christ takes part with you, and is so far from being provoked against you, as all his anger is turned upon your sin to ruin it; yes, his pity is increased the more towards you, even as the heart of a father is to a child that has some loathsome disease, or as one is to a member of his body that has leprosy, he hates not the member, for it is his flesh, but the disease, and that provokes him to pity the part affected the more. What shall not make for us,[3] when our sins, that are both against Christ and us, shall be turned as motives to him to pity us the more?

---

3   That is, what shall not be turned to our advantage and welfare.

The greater the misery is, the more is the pity when the party is beloved. Now of all miseries, sin is the greatest; and while you look at it as such, Christ will look upon it as such also. And he, loving your persons, and hating only the sin, his hatred shall all fall, and that only upon the sin, to free you of it by its ruin and destruction, but his affections shall be the more drawn out to you; and this as much when you lie under sin as under any other affliction. Therefore fear not.[4]

What is Goodwin saying here?

If you are part of Christ's own body, your sins evoke his deepest heart, his compassion and pity. He "takes part with you"—that is, he's on your side. He sides with you against your sin, not against you because of your sin. He hates sin. But he loves you. We understand this, says Goodwin, when we consider the hatred a father has against a terrible disease afflicting his child—the father hates the disease while loving the child. Indeed, at some level the presence of the disease draws out his heart to his child all the more.

This is not to ignore the disciplinary side of Christ's care for his people. The Bible clearly teaches that our sins draw forth the discipline of Christ (e.g., Heb. 12:1–11). He would not truly love us if that were not true. But even this is a reflection of his great heart for us. When a body part has been injured, it requires the pain and labor of physical therapy. But that physical therapy is not punitive; it is intended to bring healing. It is out of care for that limb that the physical therapy is assigned.

---

4 Thomas Goodwin, *The Heart of Christ* (Edinburgh: Banner of Truth, 2011), 155–56.

We'll go to a series of Old Testament texts later in this book, but let's consider one now, because it brings together several strands we've been reflecting on in this chapter, taking us deep into the heart of God that takes concrete form in Jesus. In Hosea 11 we read:

> My people are bent on turning away from me,
>> and though they call out to the Most High,
>> he shall not raise them up at all.
>
> How can I give you up, O Ephraim?
>> How can I hand you over, O Israel?
> How can I make you like Admah?
>> How can I treat you like Zeboiim?
> My heart recoils within me;
>> my compassion grows warm and tender.
> I will not execute my burning anger;
>> I will not again destroy Ephraim;
> for I am God and not a man,
>> the Holy One in your midst,
> and I will not come in wrath. (Hos. 11:7–9)

Here we have all the elements raised so far in this chapter: God's own people, amid their sinfulness, with reference to God's heart, and explicit affirmation of God's holiness. And what does the text conclude? The key observation is this: it is in consideration of his people's sins that God's heart goes out to them in compassion.

God looks at his people in all their moral filth. They have proven their waywardness time and again—not occasionally, but they "are *bent* on turning away from me" (v. 7). This is settled recalcitrance.

But here's the thing: they're his. So what happens inside of God? We must tread carefully here; God is God, and is not at the mercy of passing emotions in the way that we embodied creatures are, much less we sinful embodied creatures. But what does the text say? We are given a rare glimpse into the very center of who God is, and we see and feel the deeply affectional convulsing within the very being of God. His heart is inflamed with pity and compassion for his people. He simply cannot give them up. Nothing could cause him to abandon them. They are his.

What father could bring himself to put up for adoption his beloved son, just because his son messed up big time?

Let's not dishonor God by so emphasizing his transcendence that we lose a sense of the emotional life of God of which our own emotions are an echo, even if a fallen and distorted echo.[5] God is not a platonic ideal, immovably austere, beyond the reach of meaningful human engagement. God is free of all fallen emotion, but not all

---

5 The name theologians give to the way the Bible speaks of God's emotional life is *anthropopathism*. This is parallel to *anthropomorphism*, in which the Bible uses human terms to speak of God in ways that cannot be taken literally, such as speaking of God's "hand." Anthropopathism is a little trickier. By it we mean to protect the fact that God is not like us in our emotional fickleness; rather, he is completely perfect and transcendent and not affectable by circumstance in the way we finite humans are. He is "impassible." At the same time, we should not so write off the way the Bible speaks of God's inner life (with terms such as *anthropopathism*) that we make God a basically platonic power divorced from the welfare of his people. The key here is to understand that while nothing catches God off guard, and nothing can affect God from outside of God in a way that threatens his perfection and simplicity, he freely engages his people through a covenant relationship and he is genuinely engaged with them for their welfare. If you find the notion of divine "emotion" unhelpful, think instead (as the Puritans put it) of divine "affections"—God's heart-disposition to embrace his sinning and suffering people. To further explore the way God is both impassible and yet capable of emotion, see Rob Lister, *God Is Impassible and Impassioned: Toward a Theology of Divine Emotion* (Wheaton, IL: Crossway, 2012).

emotion (or feeling) whatsoever—where do our own emotions come from, we who are made in his image?

The text says his "compassion grows warm and tender" in light of his people's sins. Who could have imagined this is who God most deeply is? The text connects God's supreme holiness with his refusal to come in wrath. Who could have thought this up? We read:

> I am God and not a man,
>> the Holy One in your midst,
> and I will not come in wrath.

Is that what you expect God to say? Don't you actually, deep down, expect him to say the following, with one small word change?

> I am God and not a man,
>> the Holy One in your midst,
> and I will therefore come in wrath.

The Bible says that when God looks at his people's sinfulness, his transcendent holiness—his God-ness, his very divinity, that about God which makes him not us—is what makes him *unable* to come down on his people in wrath. We tend to think that because he is God and not us, the fact that he is holy renders it all the more certain that he will visit wrath on his sinful people. Once more, we are corrected; we are brought out from under our natural ways of creating God in our own image, and we allow God himself to tell us who he is.

———

Just as we so easily live with a diminished view of the punitive judgment of God that will sweep over those out of Christ, so we easily live with a diminished view of the compassionate heart of God sweeping over those in Christ. Thomas Goodwin and Hosea 11 and the sweep of the entire biblical storyline cause us to catch our breath. The sins of those who belong to God open the floodgates of his heart of compassion for us. The dam breaks. It is not our loveliness that wins his love. It is our unloveliness.

Our hearts gasp to catch up with this. It is not how the world around us works. It is not how our own hearts work. But we bow in humble submission, letting God set the terms by which he will love us.

8

To the Uttermost

He always lives to make intercession for them.

HEBREWS 7:25

ONE OF THE MORE NEGLECTED doctrines in the church today
is the heavenly intercession of Christ. When we talk about Christ's
intercession, we are talking about what Jesus is doing *now*. There
has been a remarkable recovery of the glory of what Christ did *back
then*, in his life, death, and resurrection, to save me. But what about
what he is doing now? For many of us, our functional Jesus isn't
really doing anything now; everything we need to be saved, we tend
to think, is already accomplished.

But that is not how the New Testament presents the work of
Christ. We'll spend some time considering Christ's heavenly intercession, not only because it is neglected today but also because
it is a part of Christ's work that is uniquely reflective of his heart.

As a way of framing what intercession is and its present neglect,
consider it in relation to the doctrine of justification. Much has
been written and preached and taught about this glorious doctrine

in recent years—as it should be. To be justified is to be declared righteous in the sight of God, fully legally exonerated in the divine court, based entirely on what another (Jesus) has done in our place. But our hearts are wired in such a way that we constantly drift from a moment-by-moment belief in this full exoneration. That heart resistance to complete acquittal before God based on what Christ has done became codified in medieval and then Roman Catholic theology. The Reformers such as Luther and Calvin recovered and rightly recentralized the doctrine of justification, and every generation since then has had to rediscover this doctrine afresh for themselves. It is the most counterintuitive aspect of Christianity, that we are declared right with God not once we begin to get our act together but once we collapse into honest acknowledgment that we never will.

But justification is largely a doctrine about what Christ has done in the past, rooted centrally in his death and resurrection. "Therefore, since we *have been* justified . . ." (Rom. 5:1). He died and rose again, and as we place our faith in him, we are justified, for he died the death we deserve to die.

But what is he doing now?

We don't have to speculate. The Bible tells us. He is interceding for us.

Justification is tied to what Christ did in the past. Intercession is what he is doing in the present.

Think of it this way. Christ's heart is a steady reality flowing through time. It isn't as if his heart throbbed for his people when he was on earth but has dissipated now that he is in heaven. It's not that his heart was flowing forth in a burst of mercy that took him all the way to the cross but has now cooled down, settling back once more into kindly indifference. His heart is as drawn to his people now as ever it was in his incarnate state. *And the present manifestation of his heart for his people is his constant interceding on their behalf.*

———

What is intercession?

In general terms it means that a third party comes between two others and makes a case to one on behalf of the other. Think of a parent interceding to a teacher on behalf of a child or an agent interceding to a sports franchise on behalf of an athlete.

What then does it mean for Christ to intercede? Who are the parties involved? God the Father, on the one hand, and we believers, on the other. But why would Jesus need to intercede for us? After all, haven't we been completely justified already? What is there for Christ to plead on our behalf? Hasn't he already done all that is needed to fully acquit us? In other words, does the doctrine of Christ's heavenly intercession mean that something was left incomplete in his atoning work on the cross? If we speak of the *finished* work of Christ on the cross, does the doctrine of intercession suggest that the cross was actually left unfinished?

The answer is that intercession applies what the atonement accomplished. Christ's present heavenly intercession on our behalf is a reflection of the fullness and victory and completeness of his earthly work, not a reflection of anything lacking in his earthly work. The atonement accomplished our salvation; intercession is the moment-by-moment application of that atoning work. In the past, Jesus did what he now talks about; in the present, Jesus talks about what he then did. This is why the New Testament weds justification and intercession, such as in Romans 8:33–34: "Who shall bring any charge against God's elect? It is God who justifies. Who is to condemn? Christ Jesus is the one who died—more than that, who was raised—who is at the right hand of God, who indeed is interceding for us." Intercession is the constant hitting "refresh" of our justification in the court of heaven.

Pressing in more deeply, Christ's intercession reflects how profoundly personal our rescue is. If we knew about Christ's death and resurrection but not his intercession, we would be tempted to view our salvation in overly formulaic terms. It would feel more mechanical than is true to who Christ actually is. His interceding for us reflects his heart—the same heart that carried him through life and down into death on behalf of his people is the heart that now manifests itself in constant pleading with and reminding and prevailing upon his Father to always welcome us.

This does not mean the Father is reluctant to embrace us, or that the Son has a more loving disposition toward us than the Father does. (We'll consider this more fully in chapter 14.) The atoning work of the Son was something the Father and the Son delightedly agreed to together in eternity past. The Son's intercession does not reflect the coolness of the Father but the sheer warmth of the Son. Christ does not intercede because the Father's heart is tepid toward us but because the Son's heart is so full toward us. But the Father's own deepest delight is to say yes to the Son's pleading on our behalf.

Think of an older brother cheering on his younger brother in a track meet. Even if, in that final stretch, the younger brother is well out ahead and will certainly win the race, does the older brother sit back, quiet, complacently satisfied? Not at all—he's yelling at the top of his lungs exclamations of encouragement, of affirmation, of celebration, of victory, of solidarity. He cannot be quieted. So with our own older brother.

John Bunyan wrote a whole book on Christ's heavenly intercession called *Christ a Complete Savior*. At one point he explains how the doctrine of intercession is a matter of Christ's heart. There is an objective side to our salvation, which Bunyan puts in terms of justification: God "justifies us, not either by giving laws unto us, or by becoming our example, or by our following of him in any sense, but by his blood shed for us. He justifies by bestowing upon us, not by expecting from us."[1] But added to this objective side of the gospel is a subjective reality, and notice how Bunyan puts it:

> As you must know him, and how men are justified by him, so you must know the readiness that is in him to receive and to do for those what they need that come unto God by him. Suppose his merits were [completely] efficacious, yet if it could be proved that there is a loathness in him that these merits should be bestowed upon the coming ones, there would but few adventure to wait upon him. But now, as he is full, he is free. Nothing pleases him better than to give what he has away; than to bestow it upon the poor and needy.[2]

Even if we believed fully in the doctrine of justification and knew all our sins were totally forgiven, we would not come to Christ gladly if he were an austere Savior. But his posture right now as he is in heaven, his disposition, his deepest desire, is to pour his heart

1   *The Works of John Bunyan*, ed. George Offor, 3 vols. (repr., Edinburgh: Banner of Truth, 1991), 1:221.
2   *Works of John Bunyan*, 1:221.

out on our behalf before the Father. The intercession of Christ is his heart connecting our heart to the Father's heart.

———

That text on which Bunyan based *Christ a Complete Savior*, Hebrews 7:25, is perhaps the key text in all the New Testament on the doctrine of Christ's intercession. After reflecting on Christ's abiding, permanent priesthood, the writer concludes:

> Consequently, he is able to save to the uttermost those who draw near to God through him, since he always lives to make intercession for them.

The phrase "to the uttermost" is one Greek word (*panteles*). It's a word denoting comprehensiveness, completeness, exhaustive wholeness. The only other place it is used in the New Testament is Luke 13:11, where it describes a woman who cannot stand up straight "all the way" but has been disabled for eighteen years.

What is the point of saying Christ saves "to the uttermost"? We who know our hearts understand. We are to-the-uttermost sinners. We need a to-the-uttermost Savior.

Christ doesn't merely help us. He saves us. This may seem obvious to those of us who have been walking with the Lord for some time. Of course Jesus saves us. But consider how your heart works. Do you not find within yourself an unceasing low-grade impulse to strengthen his saving work through your own contribution? We tend to operate as if Hebrews 7:25 says that Jesus "is able to save *for the most part* those who draw near to God through him." But the salvation Christ brings is *panteles*; it is comprehensive. In the flow of thought in Hebrews 7, there appears to be a special focus on the *time* aspect of this salvation. Because Jesus "holds his priesthood permanently" and "continues forever" in it (v. 24), unlike previous priests who all died (v. 23), Christ "is able to save to the uttermost." Our presence in God's good favor and family will never sputter and die, like an engine running out of gas.

We all tend to have some small pocket of our life where we have difficulty believing the forgiveness of God reaches. We *say* we are totally forgiven. And we sincerely believe our sins are forgiven. Pretty much, anyway. But there's that one deep, dark part of our lives, even our present lives, that seems so intractable, so ugly, so beyond recovery. "To the uttermost" in Hebrews 7:25 means: God's forgiving, redeeming, restoring touch reaches down into the darkest crevices of our souls, those places where we are most ashamed, most defeated. More than this: those crevices of sin are themselves the places where Christ loves us the most. His heart willingly goes there. His heart is *most* strongly drawn there. He knows us to the uttermost, and he saves us to the uttermost, because his heart is drawn out to us to the uttermost. We cannot sin our way out of his tender care.

But how do we know? The text tells us. "He is able to save to the uttermost those who draw near to God through him, *since he always lives to make intercession for them.*" Christ's heavenly intercession is the reason we know that he will save us to the uttermost.

Here's what this means. The divine Son never ceases (note the word "always") to bring his atoning life, death, and resurrection before his Father in a moment-by-moment way. Christ "turns the Father's eyes to his own righteousness," wrote Calvin, "to avert his gaze from our sins. He so reconciles the Father's heart to us that by his intercession he prepares a way and access for us to the Father's throne."[3] Do we realize what this means? Note the blessed realism of the Bible. This is the explicit acknowledgment that we Christians are ongoing sinners. Christ continues to intercede on our behalf in heaven because we continue to fail here on earth. He does not forgive us through his work on the cross and then hope we make it the rest of the way. Picture a glider, pulled up into the sky by an airplane, soon to be released to float down to earth. We are that glider; Christ is the plane. But he never disengages. He never lets go, wishing us well, hoping we can glide the rest of the way into heaven. He carries us all the way.

One way to think of Christ's intercession, then, is simply this: Jesus is praying for you right now. "It is a consoling thought," wrote theologian Louis Berkhof, "that Christ is praying for us, even when we are negligent in our prayer life."[4] Our prayer life stinks most of the time. But what if you heard Jesus praying aloud for you in the next room? Few things would calm us more deeply.

The doctrine of the present heavenly intercession of Christ is neglected today. That is too bad, because it is a consoling truth and flows right out of the heart of Christ. Whereas the doctrine of the atonement reassures us with what Christ has done in the past, the doctrine of his intercession reassures us with what he is doing in the present.

If you are in Christ, you have an intercessor, a present-day mediator, one who is happily celebrating with his Father the abundant

3   John Calvin, *Institutes of the Christian Religion*, ed. John T. McNeill, trans. Ford L. Battles, 2 vols. (Louisville, KY: Westminster John Knox, 1960), 2.16.16.
4   Louis Berkhof, *Systematic Theology* (Edinburgh: Banner of Truth, 1958), 400.

reason for both to embrace you into their deepest heart. Richard Sibbes wrote:

> What a comfort it is now in our daily approach to God to minister boldness to us in all our suits, that we go to God in the name of one that he loves, in whom his soul delights, that we have a friend in court, a friend in heaven for us, that is at the right hand of God, and interposes himself there for us, in all our suits that makes us acceptable, that perfumes our prayers and makes them acceptable. . . . Be sure therefore in all our suits to God to take along our elder brother. . . . God looks upon us, lovely in him and delights in us, as we are members of him.[5]

Our sinning goes to the uttermost. But his saving goes to the uttermost. And his saving always outpaces and overwhelms our sinning, because he always lives to intercede for us.

---

5   Richard Sibbes, *A Description of Christ*, in *The Works of Richard Sibbes*, ed. A. B. Grosart, 7 vols. (Edinburgh: Banner of Truth, 1983), 1:13.

9

An Advocate

We have an advocate with the Father,
Jesus Christ the righteous.

1 JOHN 2:1

A CLOSELY RELATED NOTION to intercession is that of advocacy.
The two ideas overlap, but there is a slightly different nuance to the
Greek words underlying each. Intercession has the idea of mediating
between two parties, bringing them together. Advocacy is similar but
has the idea of aligning oneself with another. An intercessor stands
between two parties; an advocate doesn't simply stand in between the
two parties but steps over and joins the one party as he approaches
the other. Jesus is not only an intercessor but an advocate. And like
intercession, advocacy is a neglected teaching in the church today,
and it flows straight from the depths of Christ's very heart.

Bunyan wrote a book on Hebrews 7:25, the key text for Christ's
heavenly intercession; he also wrote one on 1 John 2:1, the key text
for Christ's heavenly advocacy, which reads:

My little children, I am writing these things to you so that you may not sin. But if anyone does sin, we have an advocate with the Father, Jesus Christ the righteous.

The New Testament's message of grace is not morally indifferent. The gospel calls us to leave sin. John explicitly says that he wrote this letter so that his readers "may not sin." And if that was the sole message of the letter, that would be a valid and appropriate summons. But it would crush us. We need not only exhortation but liberation. We need not only Christ as a king but Christ as a friend. Not only over us but next to us. And that's what the rest of the verse gives us.

But if anyone does sin, we have an advocate with the Father, Jesus Christ the righteous.

———

The Greek word translated in 1 John 2:1 as "advocate" (*parakletos*) is used five times in the New Testament. The other four are all found in the Upper Room Discourse in John 14–16, each time referring to the ministry of the Holy Spirit after Jesus ascends to heaven (14:16, 26; 15:26; 16:7). It's difficult to capture the meaning of *parakletos* with just one English word. The difficulty is reflected in the diversity of translations, including "Helper" (ESV, NKJV, GNB, NASB), "Advocate" (NIV, NET), "Counselor" (CSB, RSV), "Comforter" (KJV), and "Companion" (CEB). Many of these translations contain a textual footnote giving alternate renderings, reflecting the difficulty of capturing *parakletos* with one English word. The idea is that of someone who appears on behalf of another; perhaps "advocate" comes closest of all our English words in expressing the role of a *parakletos*. (Early theologians such as Tertullian and

Augustine writing in Latin frequently translated *parakletos* in the New Testament with *advocatus*.[1])

The text of 1 John goes on immediately to say that Jesus is also "the propitiation for our sins" (1 John 2:2). Jesus as our "propitiation" means that he assuages or turns away the just wrath of the Father toward our sins. It is a legal term, an objective one. Christ as our advocate may have a faint legal connotation but more frequently in literature outside the New Testament in early times it has to do with something more subjective, expressing deep solidarity. Jesus shares with us in our actual experience. He feels what we feel. He draws near. And he speaks up longingly on our behalf.

Who is this advocate for? The text tells us: "anyone." The only qualification needed is desire.

When will we receive this advocacy? The text tells us: it does not say "we will have an advocate" but "we have an advocate." All those in Christ have, right now, someone speaking on their behalf.

Why is this advocate able to help us? The text tells us: he is "righteous." He and he alone. We are unrighteous; he is righteous. Even our best repenting of our sin is itself plagued with more sin needing more forgiveness. To come to the Father without an advocate is hopeless. To be allied with an advocate, one who came and sought me out rather than waiting for me to come to him, one who is righteous in all the ways I am not—this is calm and confidence before the Father.

---

1   F. W. Danker, ed., *A Greek-English Lexicon of the New Testament and Other Early Christian Literature*, 3rd ed. (Chicago: University of Chicago Press, 2000), 766.

Let's look more deeply at the difference between Christ's intercession and his advocacy by noting the difference between Hebrews
7:25 and 1 John 2:1. Hebrews 7:25 says that Christ always lives to
make intercession for us, whereas 1 John 2:1 says, "If anyone does
sin, we have an advocate."

Do you see the difference? Intercession is something Christ is
always doing, while advocacy is something he does as occasion calls
for it. Apparently he intercedes for us given our general sinfulness,
but he advocates for us in the case of specific sins. Bunyan explains
it like this:

> Christ, as Priest, goes before, and Christ, as an Advocate, comes
> after.
>
> Christ, as Priest, continually intercedes; Christ, as Advocate,
> in case of great transgressions, pleads.
>
> Christ, as Priest, has need to act always, but Christ, as Advocate,
> sometimes only.
>
> Christ, as Priest, acts in time of peace; but Christ, as Advocate,
> in times of broils, turmoils, and sharp contentions; wherefore,
> Christ, as Advocate, is, as I may call him, a reserve, and his time
> is then to arise, to stand up and plead, when his own are clothed
> with some filthy sin that of late they have fallen into.[2]

Note the *personal* nature of Christ's advocacy. It is not a static part
of his work. His advocacy rears up when occasion requires it. The
Bible nowhere teaches that once we have been savingly united with
Christ, we will find grievous sins to be a thing of the past. On the

---

2   John Bunyan, *The Work of Jesus Christ as an Advocate*, in *The Works of John Bunyan*, ed.
    G. Offor, 3 vols. (repr., Edinburgh: Banner of Truth, 1991), 1:169.

contrary, it is our regenerate state that has more deeply sensitized us to the impropriety of our sins. Our sins feel far more sinful after we have become believers than before. And it's not only our felt perception of our sinfulness; we do indeed continue to sin after becoming believers. Sometimes we sin big sins. And that's what Christ's advocacy is for. It's God way of encouraging us not to throw in the towel. Yes, we fail Christ as his disciples. But his advocacy on our behalf rises higher than our sins. His advocacy speaks louder than our failures. All is taken care of.

When you sin, remember your legal standing before God because of the work of Christ; but remember also your advocate before God because of the heart of Christ. He rises up and defends your cause, based on the merits of his own sufferings and death. Your salvation is not merely a matter of a saving formula, but of a saving person. When you sin, his strength of resolve rises all the higher. When his brothers and sisters fail and stumble, he advocates on their behalf *because it is who he is.* He cannot bear to leave us alone to fend for ourselves.

———

Consider your own life. How do you think about Jesus's attitude toward that dark pocket of your life that only you know? The over-dependence upon alcohol. The lost temper, time and again. The shady business about your finances. The inveterate people-pleasing that looks to others like niceness but which you know to be fear of man. The entrenched resentment that bursts out in behind-the-back accusations. The habitual use of pornography.

Who *is* Jesus, in those moments of spiritual blankness? Not: Who is he once you conquer that sin, but who is he in the midst of it? The apostle John says: he stands up and defies all accusers. "Satan had the first word, but Christ the last," wrote Bunyan. "Satan must be speechless after a plea of our Advocate."[3] Jesus is our Paraclete, our comforting defender, the one nearer than we know, and his heart is such that he stands and speaks in our defense *when* we sin, not after we get over it. In that sense his advocacy is itself our conquering of it.

We are indeed called to forsake our sins, and no healthy Christian would suggest otherwise. When we choose to sin, we forsake our true identity as a child of God, we invite misery into our lives, and we displease our heavenly Father. We are called to mature into deeper levels of personal holiness as we walk with the Lord, truer consecration, new vistas of obedience. But when we don't—when we choose to sin—though we forsake our true identity, our Savior does not forsake us. These are the very moments when his heart erupts on our behalf in renewed advocacy in heaven with a resounding defense that silences all accusations, astonishes the angels, and celebrates the Father's embrace of us in spite of all our messiness.

What kind of Christian does this doctrine create?

Fallen humans are natural self-advocates. It flows out of us. Self-exonerating, self-defending. We do not need to teach young children to make excuses when they are caught misbehaving. There is a natural built-in mechanism that immediately kicks into gear to explain why it wasn't really their fault. Our fallen hearts intuitively manufacture reasons that our case is not really that bad. The fall is manifested not only in our sinning but in our response to our sinning. We minimize, we excuse, we explain

3 Bunyan, *Works of John Bunyan*, 1:194.

away. In short, we speak, even if only in our hearts, in our defense. We advocate for ourselves.

What if we never needed to advocate for ourselves because another had undertaken to do so? What if that advocate knew exhaustively just how fallen we are, and yet at the same time was able to make a better defense for us than we ever could? No blame shifting or excuses, the way our self-advocacies tend to operate, but perfectly just, pointing to his all-sufficient sacrifice and sufferings on the cross in our place? We would be free. Free of the need to defend ourselves, to bolster our sense of worth through self-contribution, to quietly parade before others our virtues in painful subconscious awareness of our inferiorities and weaknesses. We can leave our case to be made by Christ, the only righteous one.

Bunyan puts it best:

Christ gave for us the price of blood; but that is not all; Christ as a Captain has conquered death and the grave for us, but that is not all; Christ as a Priest intercedes for us in heaven; but that is not all. Sin is still in us, and with us, and mixes itself with whatever we do, whether what we do be religious or civil; for not only our prayers and our sermons, our hearings and preaching; but our houses, our shops, our trades, and our beds, are all polluted with sin.

Nor does the devil, our night and day adversary, forbear to tell our bad deeds to our Father, urging that we might forever be disinherited for this.

But what should we now do, if we had not an Advocate; yes, if we had not one who would plead; yes, if we had not one that could prevail, and that would faithfully execute that office for us? Why, we must die.

But since we are rescued by him, let us, as to ourselves, lay our hand upon our mouth, and be silent.[4]

Do not minimize your sin or excuse it away. Raise no defense. Simply take it to the one who is already at the right hand of the Father, advocating for you on the basis of his own wounds. Let your own unrighteousness, in all your darkness and despair, drive you to Jesus Christ, the righteous, in all his brightness and sufficiency.

---

4 Bunyan, *Works of John Bunyan*, 1:197.

10

The Beauty of the Heart of Christ

Whoever loves father or mother more
than me is not worthy of me.
MATTHEW 10:37

IN THE SUMMER OF 1740 Jonathan Edwards preached a sermon exclusively to the children in his congregation, those from ages one through fourteen. Picture the great theologian, preparing in his study there in Northampton, Massachusetts, considering what to say to the six- and eight- and ten-year-olds in his church. The sermon as he prepared it covered twelve small pages with his fine, flowery, handwritten script. The top of the first page simply read: "To the children, Aug. 1740."

What would you expect the greatest theologian in American history to say to the kids in his congregation? Here was Edwards's main point: "Children ought to love the Lord Jesus Christ above all things in the world."[1]

---

1   Jonathan Edwards, "Children Ought to Love the Lord Jesus Christ Above All," in *The Works of Jonathan Edwards*, vol. 22, *Sermons and Discourses 1739–1742*, ed. Harry S. Stout and Nathan O. Hatch (New Haven, CT: Yale University Press, 2003), 171.

He took as his text Matthew 10:37, which in his King James Version read, "He that loveth father or mother more than me is not worthy of me." It was a short sermon, taking perhaps fifteen or twenty minutes to preach. In it Edwards lists six reasons that children should love Jesus more than anything else in life. The first is:

> There is no love so great and so wonderful as that which is in the heart of Christ. He is one that delights in mercy; he is ready to pity those that are in suffering and sorrowful circumstances; one that delights in the happiness of his creatures. The love and grace that Christ has manifested does as much exceed all that which is in this world as the sun is brighter than a candle. Parents are often full of kindness towards their children, but that is no kindness like Jesus Christ's.

The first thing out of Jonathan Edwards's mouth, in exhorting the kids in his church to love Jesus more than everything else this world can offer, is the heart of Christ. And in this sermon and throughout his writings more broadly, Edwards takes us in a different direction than Goodwin and other theologians have tended to go. When Edwards talks about Christ's heart, he often emphasizes the beauty or loveliness of his gracious heart. And that's worth a chapter.

———

Look again at what Edwards says: "There is no love so great and so wonderful as that which is in the heart of Christ."

Human beings are created with a built-in pull toward beauty. We are arrested by it. Edwards understood this deeply and saw that this magnetic pull toward beauty also occurs in spiritual things—in fact, Edwards would say that it is spiritual beauty of which every other beauty is a shadow or echo. Throughout his ministry Edwards sought to woo people with the beauty of Christ, and that is all he is doing with the kids in his church in August of 1740. Later in this sermon he remarks: "Everything that is lovely in God is in Christ, and everything that is or can be lovely in any man is in him: for he is man as well as God, and he is the holiest, meekest, most humble, and every way the most excellent man that ever was."[2]

Any possible loveliness is in Jesus, because "he is the holiest, meekest, most humble, and every way the most excellent man that ever was." This language of Christ's meekness and humility are the very way Christ himself describes his own heart in Matthew 11:29. In other words, it is Christ's gentle heart that adorns him with beauty; or put the other way, what most deeply attracts us to Christ is his gentle, tender, humble heart.

In our churches today we often refer to the glory of God and the glory of Christ. But what is it about God's glory that draws us in and causes us to conquer our sins and makes us radiant people? Is it the sheer size of God, a consideration of the immensity of the universe and thus of the Creator, a sense of God's transcendent greatness, that pulls us toward him? No, Edwards would say; it is the loveliness of his heart. It is, he says, a "sight of the divine beauty of Christ, that bows the wills, and draws the hearts of men. A sight of the greatness of God in his attributes, may overwhelm men." But seeing God's greatness is not our deepest need, but seeing his goodness. Seeing only his greatness, "the enmity and opposition of the heart, may remain in its full strength, and the will remain inflexible; whereas, one glimpse of the moral and spiritual glory of God, and supreme

2   Edwards, *Works*, 22:172.

amiableness of Jesus Christ, shining into the heart, overcomes and abolishes this opposition, and inclines the soul to Christ, as it were, by an omnipotent power."[3]

We are drawn to God by the beauty of the heart of Jesus. When sinners and sufferers come to Christ, Edwards says in another sermon, "the person that they find is exceeding excellent and lovely." For they come to one who is not only "of excellent majesty and of perfect purity and brightness," but also one in whom this majesty is "conjoined with the sweetest grace, one that clothes himself with mildness and meekness and love."[4] Jesus is "exceeding ready to receive them." Given their sinfulness, they are shocked to find that their sins cause him to be all the more ready to plunge them into his heart. "They unexpectedly find him with open arms to embrace them, ready forever to forget all their sins as though they had never been."[5]

In other words, when we come to Christ, we are startled by the beauty of his welcoming heart. The surprise is itself what draws us in.

———

Have we considered the loveliness of the heart of Christ?

Perhaps beauty is not a category that comes naturally to mind when we think about Christ. Maybe we think of God and Christ

3 Jonathan Edwards, "True Grace, Distinguished from the Experience of Devils," in *The Works of Jonathan Edwards*, vol. 25, *Sermons and Discourses, 1743–1758*, ed. Wilson H. Kimnach (New Haven, CT: Yale University Press, 2006), 635.

4 Jonathan Edwards, "Seeking After Christ," in *The Works of Jonathan Edwards*, vol. 22, *Sermons and Discourses, 1739–1742*, ed. Harry S. Stout and Nathan O. Hatch (New Haven, CT: Yale University Press, 2003), 289.

5 Edwards, *Works of Jonathan Edwards*, 22:290.

in terms of truth, not beauty. But the whole reason we care about sound doctrine is for the sake of preserving God's beauty, just as the whole reason we care about effective focal lenses on a camera is to capture with precision the beauty we photograph.

Let Jesus draw you in through the loveliness of his heart. This is a heart that upbraids the impenitent with all the harshness that is appropriate, yet embraces the penitent with more openness than we are able to feel. It is a heart that walks us into the bright meadow of the felt love of God. It is a heart that drew the despised and forsaken to his feet in self-abandoning hope. It is a heart of perfect balance and proportion, never overreacting, never excusing, never lashing out. It is a heart that throbs with desire for the destitute. It is a heart that floods the suffering with the deep solace of shared solidarity in that suffering. It is a heart that is gentle and lowly.

So let the heart of Jesus be something that is not only gentle toward you but lovely to you. If I may put it this way: *romance* the heart of Jesus. All I mean is, ponder him through his heart. Allow yourself to be allured. Why not build in to your life unhurried quiet, where, among other disciplines, you consider the radiance of who he actually is, what animates him, what his deepest delight is? Why not give your soul room to be reenchanted with Christ time and again?

When you look at the glorious older saints in your church, how do you think they got there? Sound doctrine, yes. Resolute obedience, without a doubt. Suffering without becoming cynical, for sure. But maybe another reason, maybe the deepest reason, is that they have, over time, been won over in their deepest affections to a gentle Savior. Perhaps they have simply tasted, over many years, the surprise of a Christ for whom their very sins draw him in rather than push him away. Maybe they have not only known that Jesus loved them but felt it.

———

We can't close this chapter without thinking about the children in our lives. Jonathan Edwards told the kids he knew, "There is no love so great and so wonderful as that which is in the heart of Christ." How might we, in our own way and time, do the same?

What is it that the children whom we greet in the hallways of our church need? Most deeply? Yes, they need friends, and encouragement, and academic support, and good square meals. But might it be that the truest need, the thing that will sustain and oxygenate them when all these other vital needs go unmet, is a sense of the attractiveness of who Jesus is for them? How he actually feels about them?

With our own kids, if we are parents, what's our job? That question could be answered with a hundred valid responses. But at the center, our job is to show our kids that even our best love is a shadow of a greater love. To put a sharper edge on it: to make the tender heart of Christ irresistible and unforgettable. Our goal is that our kids would leave the house at eighteen and be unable to live the rest of their lives believing that their sins and sufferings repel Christ.

This is perhaps the greatest gift my own dad has given me. He taught my siblings and me sound doctrine as we were growing up, to be sure—which is itself a sore neglect across evangelical family life today. But there's something he has shown me that runs even deeper than truth about God, and that is the heart of God, proven in Christ, the friend of sinners. Dad made that heart beautiful to me. He didn't crowbar me into that; he drew me in. We too have the privilege of finding creative ways of drawing in the kids all around us to the heart of Jesus. His desire to draw near to sinners and sufferers is not only doctrinally true but aesthetically attractive.

11

The Emotional Life of Christ

When Jesus saw her weeping, and the Jews who
had come with her also weeping, he was deeply
moved in his spirit and greatly troubled.

JOHN 11:33

ONE OF THE DOCTRINES in the area of Christology that is difficult for some Christians to fully grasp is the permanent humanity of Christ. The impression often seems to be that the Son of God came down from heaven in incarnate form, spent three decades or so as a human, and then returned to heaven to revert back to his preincarnate state.

But this is Christological error, if not outright heresy. The Son of God clothed himself with humanity and will never unclothe himself. He became a man and always will be. This is the significance of the doctrine of Christ's ascension: he went into heaven with the very body, reflecting his full humanity, that was raised out of the tomb. He is and always has been divine as well, of course. But his humanity, once taken on, will never end. In Christ, the Heidelberg Catechism says, "we have our own flesh in heaven" (Q. 49).

One implication of this truth of Christ's permanent humanity is that when we see the feeling and passions and affections of the incarnate Christ toward sinners and sufferers as given to us in the four Gospels, *we are seeing who Jesus is for us today*. The Son has not retreated back into the disembodied divine state in which he existed before he took on flesh.

And that flesh that the Son took on was true, full, complete humanity. Indeed, Jesus was more truly human than anyone who has ever lived. Ancient heresies such as Eutychianism (also called Monophysitism) viewed Jesus as a sort of blend between the human and the divine, a unique third kind of being somewhere in between God and man—heresies that were condemned at the fourth ecumenical council in Chalcedon (in modern-day Turkey) in AD 451. The Chalcedonian creed that came out of that council speaks of Jesus as "truly God and truly man" rather than a reduced blend of both. Whatever it means to be human (and to be human without sin), Jesus was and is. And emotions are an essential part of being human. Our emotions are diseased by the fall, of course, just as every part of fallen humanity is affected by the fall. But emotions are not themselves a result of the fall. Jesus experienced the full range of emotions that we do (Heb. 2:17; 4:15).[1] As Calvin put it, "the Son of God having clothed himself with our flesh, of his own accord clothed himself also with human feelings, so that he did not differ at all from his brethren, sin only excepted."[2]

---

1   B. B. Warfield, *The Person and Work of Christ* (Oxford, UK: Benediction Classics, 2015), 137–38.

2   John Calvin, *Commentary on the Gospel according to John*, vol. 1, trans. William Pringle (Grand Rapids, MI: Baker, 2003), 440.

The great Princeton theologian B. B. Warfield (1851–1921) wrote a famous essay in 1912 called "On the Emotional Life of Our Lord." In it he explored what the Gospels reveal about Christ's inner life, what Warfield calls his "emotional" life. Warfield did not mean what we often mean by the word *emotional*—imbalanced, reactionary, driven by our feelings in an unhealthy way. He simply is noticing what Jesus *felt*. And as he reflects on Christ's emotions, Warfield notes repeatedly the way his emotions flow from his deepest heart.

What then do we see in the Gospels of the emotional life of Jesus? What does a godly emotional life look like? It is an inner life of perfect balance, proportion, and control, on the one hand; but also of extensive depth of feeling, on the other hand.

Warfield reflects on various emotions that we see reflected in Jesus in the Gospels. Two of these, compassion and anger, are explored in a way that fills out our own study on the heart of Christ.

—

Warfield begins his study of specific emotions in the life of Christ this way:

> The emotion which we should naturally expect to find most frequently attributed to that Jesus whose whole life was a mission of mercy, and whose ministry was so marked by deeds of beneficence that it was summed up in the memory of his followers as a going through the land "doing good" (Acts 10:38), is no doubt "compassion." In point of fact, this is the emotion which is most frequently attributed to him.[3]

3 Warfield, *Person and Work of Christ*, 96.

He then goes on to cite specific examples of Christ's compassion. Throughout, he is trying to help us see that Jesus did not simply operate in deeds of compassion but actually felt the inner turmoils and roiling emotions of pity toward the unfortunate. When the blind and the lame and the afflicted appealed to Jesus, "his heart responded with a profound feeling of pity for them. His compassion fulfilled itself in the outward act; but what is emphasized by the term employed to express our Lord's response is . . . the profound internal movement of his emotional nature."[4] Hearing the plea, for example, of two blind men for sight (Matt. 20:30–31) or that of the leper for cleansing (Mark 1:40), or simply seeing (without hearing any plea) a distressed widow (Luke 7:12), "set our Lord's heart throbbing with pity."[5]

In each of these instances Jesus is described as acting out of the same internal state (Matt. 20:34; Mark 1:41; Luke 7:13). The Greek word is *splanchnizo*, which is often rendered as "to have compassion." But the word denotes more than passing pity; it refers to a depth of feeling in which your feelings and longings churn within you. The noun form of this verb means, most literally, one's guts or intestines.

Warfield is particularly insightful, however, on the implication of this compassion for how we understand who Jesus was and what his inner emotional life was actually like. Throughout his essay Warfield reflects on the fact that Jesus is the one perfect human ever to walk the face of the earth; how, then, are we to understand his emotional life, and an emotion such as compassion? What he helps us see is that Christ's emotions outstrip our own in depth of

4 Warfield, *Person and Work of Christ*, 97–98.
5 Warfield, *Person and Work of Christ*, 98.

feeling, because he was truly human (as opposed to a divine-human blend) and because he was a perfect human.

Perhaps an example would clarify. I remember walking the streets of Bangalore, India, a few years ago. I had just finished preaching at a church in town and was waiting for my ride to arrive. Immediately outside the church grounds was an older man, apparently homeless, sitting in a large cardboard box. His clothes were tattered and dirty. He was missing several teeth. And what was immediately most distressing was his hands. Most of his fingers were partially eaten away. It was clear they hadn't been damaged by an injury but had simply been eaten away over time. He was a leper.

What happened in my heart in that moment? My fallen, prone-to-wander heart? Compassion. A little, anyway. But it was tepid compassion. The fall has ruined me, all of me, including my emotions. Fallen emotions not only sinfully overreact; they also sinfully underreact. Why was my heart so cool toward this miserable gentleman? Because I am a sinner.

What then must it mean for a sinless man with fully functioning emotions to lay eyes on that leper? Sin restrained my emotions of compassion; what would unrestrained emotions of compassion be like?

That is what Jesus felt. Perfect, unfiltered compassion. What must that have been like, rising up within him? What would perfect pity look like, mediated not through a prophetic oracle as in the Old Testament but through an actual, real human? And what if that human were still a human, though now in heaven, and looked at each of us spiritual lepers with unfiltered compassion, an outflowing affection not limited by the sinful self-absorption that restricts our own compassion?

———

And not only compassion. What would perfect anger look like?

This is perhaps the key contribution of Warfield's seminal essay, and it may map on to a rising question in your own mind in the course of this study of the heart of Christ. Namely, how does this emphasis on Christ's heart, his gentle and lowly heart, his deep compassion, fit with the episodes of anger that we find in the Gospels? Are we being unhelpfully partial if we focus on his gentleness? Is he not also wrathful?

Consider what Warfield says as he begins to explore the anger of Jesus. After noting that it is a matter of moral perfection not only to distinguish between good and evil but to be positively drawn toward one and repelled by the other, he says:

> It would be impossible, therefore, for a moral being to stand in the presence of perceived wrong indifferent and unmoved. Precisely what we mean by a moral being is a being perceptive of the difference between right and wrong and reacting appropriately to right and wrong perceived as such. The emotions of indignation and anger belong therefore to the very self-expression of a moral being as such and cannot be lacking to him in the presence of wrong.[6]

Warfield is saying that a morally perfect human such as Christ would be a contradiction if he *didn't* get angry. Perhaps we feel that to the degree we emphasize Christ's compassion, we neglect his anger; and to the degree we emphasize his anger, we neglect his compassion. But what we must see is that the two rise and fall

6   Warfield, *Person and Work of Christ*, 107.

together. A compassion-less Christ could never have gotten angry at the injustices all around him, the severity and human barbarity, even that flowing from the religious elite. No, "compassion and indignation rise together in his soul."[7] It is the father who loves his daughter most whose anger rises most fiercely if she is mistreated.

Consider Jesus's anger through the following logical syllogism:

Premise #1: Moral goodness revolts with indignant anger against evil.

Premise #2: Jesus was the epitome of moral goodness; he was morally perfect.

Conclusion: Jesus revolted against evil with indignant anger more deeply than anyone.

Yes, Jesus pronounced searing denunciations on those who cause children to sin, saying it would be a better fate if they were drowned (Matt. 18:6), not because he gleefully enjoys torturing the wicked but most deeply because he loves little children. It is his heart of love, not a gleeful exacting of justice, that rises up from his soul to elicit such a fearsome pronouncement of woe.

Likewise with the sustained pronouncement of judgment on the scribes and Pharisees throughout Matthew 23—what fuels such terrifying censures? It is his concern for those being misled and mistreated by these revered religious PhDs. Those who listen to these teachers are being given "heavy burdens, hard to bear" (Matt. 23:4). These dear people are being made "twice as much a child of hell" as the scribes and Pharisees are (23:15). In short, the scribes and Pharisees are guilty of the blood of a whole string

---

7   Warfield, *Person and Work of Christ*, 141.

of righteous prophets (23:34–35). Their heart for the people was the opposite of Jesus's heart. They wished to use the people, to build themselves up; Jesus wished to serve the people, to build them up. Jesus wanted to gather the people under his wings the way a mother hen gathers her chicks under her wings for maternal protection (23:37).

What about driving the money changers out of the temple? That wasn't exactly a very gentle thing to do. How does his heart fit with that? We're actually told that Jesus made the whip himself (John 2:15). Picture him there, off alone, weaving back and forth, calmly constructing the weapon by which he would ferociously drive out the money changers, flipping over their tables. But why did he do this? Because they had perverted the use of the temple. This was the house of God, the one place where sinners could come and offer sacrifices and enjoy fellowship with God, reassurance of his favor and grace. It was to be a place of prayer, of blessed interchange between God and his people. The money changers were the ones doing the real overturning—overturning the temple from a place to know and see God to a place to make money.

What we are saying is that, yes, Christ got angry and still gets angry, for he is the perfect human, who loves too much to remain indifferent. And this righteous anger reflects his heart, his tender compassion. But because his deepest heart is tender compassion, he is the quickest to get angry and feels anger most furiously—and all without a hint of sin tainting that anger.

The clearest example of Christ's righteous anger in the Gospels is the death of Lazarus in John 11, where the verb used in verses 33 and 38 to describe Jesus's inner state is one of profound fury. "Jesus approached the grave of Lazarus, in a state, not of uncontrollable grief, but of irrepressible anger. . . . The emotion which tore his breast and clamored for utterance was just rage."[8] Warfield goes on to consider the role that the Lazarus episode plays in John's Gospel as a whole. Note the way he ties in the heart of Christ:

> Inextinguishable fury seizes upon him. . . . It is death that is the object of his wrath, and behind death him who has the power of death, and whom he has come into the world to destroy. Tears of sympathy may fill his eyes, but this is incidental. His soul is held by rage. . . . The raising of Lazarus thus becomes, not an isolated marvel, but . . . a decisive instance and open symbol of Jesus' conquest of death and hell.
>
> What John does for us . . . is to uncover for us the heart of Jesus, as he wins for us our salvation. Not in cold unconcern, but in flaming wrath against the foe, Jesus smites in our behalf. He has not only saved us from the evils which oppress us; he has felt for and with us in our oppression, and under the impulse of these feelings has wrought out our redemption.[9]

While Christ is a lion to the impenitent, he is a lamb to the penitent—the reduced, the open, the hungry, the desiring, the confessing, the self-effacing. He hates with righteous hatred all that plagues you. Remember that Isaiah 53 speaks of Christ bearing our griefs and carrying our sorrows (v. 4). He wasn't only punished in

---

8 Warfield, *Person and Work of Christ*, 115.
9 Warfield, *Person and Work of Christ*, 117. See also the comments of Calvin, explicitly disagreeing with Augustine and proleptically agreeing with Warfield, on the full-throttled humanness of Christ's emotions in John 11: Calvin, *Commentary on the Gospel according to John*, 1:439–43.

our place, experiencing something we never will (condemnation); he also suffered with us, experiencing what we ourselves do (mistreatment). In your grief, he is grieved. In your distress, he is distressed.

Are you angry today? Let us not be too quick to assume our anger is sinful. After all, the Bible positively orders us to be angry when occasion calls for it (Ps. 4:4; Eph. 4:26). Perhaps you have reason to be angry. Perhaps you have been sinned against, and the only appropriate response is anger. Be comforted by this: *Jesus is angry alongside you.* He joins you in your anger. Indeed, he is angrier than you could ever be about the wrong done to you. Your just anger is a shadow of his. And his anger, unlike yours, has zero taint of sin in it. As you consider those who have wronged you, let Jesus be angry on your behalf. His anger can be trusted. For it is an anger that springs from his compassion for you. The indignation he felt when he came upon mistreatment of others in the Gospels is the same indignation he feels now in heaven upon mistreatments of you.

In that knowledge, release your debtor and breathe again. Let Christ's heart for you not only wash you in his compassion but also assure you of his solidarity in rage against all that distresses you, most centrally death and hell.

12

A Tender Friend

. . . a friend of tax collectors and sinners!
MATTHEW 11:19

ONE CATEGORY IN WHICH to think about the heart of Christ is that of friendship. His heart takes shape as our never-failing friend.

This was a common way to understand Christ more in past generations than today. We consider the theme of divine friendship in the Puritans in this chapter, but we need not even retreat to historic or even Christian authors to learn that we today have lamentably impoverished the category even of friendship between humans, perhaps especially among men. Richard Godbeer, professor of history at Virginia Commonwealth University, has shown through an extensive review of written correspondence that male friendship has been greatly diluted in the present time when compared with the richness of healthy, nonerotic affection between men in colonial America.[1]

---

1 Richard Godbeer, *The Overflowing of Friendship: Love Between Men and the Creation of the American Republic* (Baltimore, MD: John Hopkins University Press, 2009).

But if we allow the world around us in our present cultural moment to dictate to us the significance of friendship, we not only lose out on a reality vital to human flourishing at the horizontal level; we lose out, even worse, on enjoying the friendship of Christ at a vertical level.

One of the most arresting references to Christ's friendship comes just before the lodestar text of our study in Matthew 11:28–30. In Matthew 11:19 Jesus quotes his accusers as contemptibly calling him "a friend of tax collectors and sinners!" (that is, a friend of the most despicable kinds of sinners known in that culture). And as is often the case in the Gospels—such as when the demons say, "I know who you are—the Holy One of God" (Mark 1:24), or when Satan himself acknowledges Christ to be "the Son of God" (Luke 4:9)—it is not his disciples but his antagonists who most clearly perceive who he is. Though the crowds call him the friend of sinners as an indictment, the label is one of unspeakable comfort for those who know themselves to be sinners. That Jesus is friend to sinners is only contemptible to those who feel themselves not to be in that category.

What does it mean that Christ is a friend to sinners? At the very least, it means that he enjoys spending time with them. It also means that they feel welcome and comfortable around him. Notice the passing line that starts off a series of parables in Luke: "Now the tax collectors and sinners were all drawing near to hear him" (Luke 15:1). The very two groups of people whom Jesus is accused of befriending in Matthew 11 are those who can't stay away from him in Luke 15. They are at ease around him. They sense something different about him. Others hold them at arms' length, but Jesus offers the enticing intrigue of fresh hope. What he is really doing, at bottom, is pulling them into his heart.

———

Consider your own relational circle. Doubtless the line of who your friends are could be drawn in varying places, like concentric circles narrowing in to a bull's-eye. There are some people in our lives whose name we know, but they're really on the periphery of our affections. Others are closer to the middle, but perhaps not intimate friends. Continuing to move toward the center, some of us are blessed to have a particularly close friend or two, someone who really knows us and "gets" us, someone for whom it is simply a mutual delight to be in each other's company. To many of us, God has given a spouse as our closest earthly friend.

Even walking through this brief thought experiment, of course, ignites pockets of mental pain. Some of us are forced to acknowledge that we do not have one true friend, someone we could go to with any problem knowing we would not be turned away. Who in our lives do we feel safe with—really safe, safe enough to open up about *everything*?

Here is the promise of the gospel and the message of the whole Bible: *In Jesus Christ, we are given a friend who will always enjoy rather than refuse our presence.* This is a companion whose embrace of us does not strengthen or weaken depending on how clean or unclean, how attractive or revolting, how faithful or fickle, we presently are. The friendliness of his heart for us subjectively is as fixed and stable as is the declaration of his justification of us objectively.

Won't most of us admit that even with our best friends, we don't feel fully comfortable divulging everything about our lives? We like them, and even love them, and go on vacation with them, and sing their praises to others—but we don't really, at the deepest heart level, *entrust* ourselves to them. Even in many of our marriages, we are friends of a sort, but we haven't gotten naked in soul the way we have in body.

What if you had a friend at the center of the bull's-eye of your relationship circle, whom you knew would never raise his eyebrows at what you share with him, even the worst parts of you? All our human friendships have a limit to what they can withstand. But what if there were a friend with no limit? No ceiling on what he would put up with and still want to be with you? "All the kinds and degrees of friendship meet in Christ," wrote Sibbes.[2]

Consider the depiction of the risen Christ in Revelation 3. There he says (to a group of Christians who are "wretched, pitiable, poor, blind, and naked," v. 17): "Behold, I stand at the door and knock. If anyone hears my voice and opens the door"—what will Christ do?—"I will come in to him and eat with him, and he with me" (v. 20). Jesus wants to come in to you—wretched, pitiable, poor, blind, naked you—and enjoy meals together. Spend time with you. Deepen the acquaintance. With a good friend, you don't need to constantly fill in all gaps of silence with words. You can just be warmly present together, quietly relishing each other's company. "Mutual communion is the soul of all true friendship," wrote Goodwin, "and a familiar converse with a friend has the greatest sweetness in it."[3]

2   Richard Sibbes, *Bowels Opened, Or, A Discovery of the Near and Dear Love, Union, and Communion Between Christ and the Church*, in *The Works of Richard Sibbes*, ed. A. B. Grosart, 7 vols. (repr., Edinburgh: Banner of Truth, 1983), 2:36.
3   Thomas Goodwin, *Of Gospel Holiness in the Heart and Life*, in *The Works of Thomas Goodwin*, 12 vols. (repr., Grand Rapids, MI: Reformation Heritage, 2006), 7:197.

We should not overly domesticate Jesus here. He is not just any friend. A few chapters earlier in Revelation we see a depiction of Christ so overwhelming to John that he falls down, immobilized (1:12–16). But neither should we dilute the humanness, the sheer relational desire, clearly present in these words from the mouth of the risen Christ himself. He isn't waiting for you to trigger his heart; he is already standing at the door, knocking, wanting to come in to you. What's our job? "Our duty," says Sibbes, "is to accept of Christ's inviting of us. What will we do for him, if we will not feast with him?"[4]

———

But not only does a true friend pursue you; he allows you to pursue him, and he opens himself up to you without holding anything back. Have you ever noticed the particular point Jesus is making when he calls his disciples "friends" in John 15? On the verge of going to the cross, Jesus tells them, "No longer do I call you servants, for the servant does not know what his master is doing; but I have called you friends, for all that I have heard from my Father I have made known to you" (John 15:15).

Jesus's friends are those to whom he has opened up his deepest purposes. Jesus says that he does not channel over to his disciples some of what the Father has told him; he tells them everything. There is nothing held back. He lets them completely in. Jesus's friends are welcome to come to him. Jonathan Edwards preached:

> God in Christ allows such little, poor creatures as you are to come to him, to love communion with him, and to maintain a

communication of love with him. You may go to God and tell him how you love him and open your heart and he will accept of it. . . . He is come down from heaven and has taken upon him the human nature in purpose, that he might be near to you and might be, as it were, your companion.[5]

Companion is another word for friend, but it specifically connotes the idea of someone who goes with you on a journey. As we make our pilgrimage through this wide wilderness of a world, we have a steady, constant friend.

What I am trying to say in this chapter is that the heart of Christ not only heals our feelings of rejection with his embrace, and not only corrects our sense of his harshness with a view of his gentleness, and not only changes our assumption of his aloofness into an awareness of his sympathy with us, but it also heals our aloneness with his sheer companionship.

In volume 2 of his *Works* Richard Sibbes reflects on what it means that Jesus Christ is our friend. Particularly striking is the common theme as he draws out several facets of the friendship of Christ to his people. That common theme is mutuality; in other words, friendship is a two-way relationship of joy, comfort, and openness,

---

5   Jonathan Edwards, "The Spirit of the True Saints Is a Spirit of Divine Love," in *The Glory and Honor of God: Volume 2 of the Previously Unpublished Sermons of Jonathan Edwards*, ed. Michael McMullen (Nashville, TN: Broadman, 2004), 339. Edwards: "There is no person in the world that stands in so endearing a relation to Christians as Christ; he is our friend and our nearest friend." *The Works of Jonathan Edwards*, vol. 10, *Sermons and Discourses 1720–1723*, ed. Wilson H. Kimnach (New Haven, CT: Yale University Press, 1992), 158. In one of his more well-known sermons, "The Excellency of Christ," Edwards mentions Christ as our friend more than thirty times. *The Works of Jonathan Edwards*, vol. 19, *Sermons and Discourses 1734–1738*, ed. M. X. Lesser (New Haven, CT: Yale University Press, 2001), 21.

that of peers, as distinct from a one-way relationship, such as in that of king to subject or parent to child. To be sure, Christ is indeed our ruler, our authority, the one to whom all allegiance and obedience are reverently due. Sibbes reminds us of that explicitly as he reflects on the friendship of Christ ("As he is our friend, so he is our king."[6]). But equally, and perhaps less obvious or intuitive to us, the condescension of God in the person of his Son means that he approaches us on our own terms and befriends us for both his and our mutual delight.

Consider the way Sibbes speaks of Christ's friendship with us:

In friendship there is a mutual consent, a union of judgment and affections. There is a mutual sympathy in the good and ill one of another. . . .

There is liberty which is the life of friendship; there is a free intercourse between friends, a free opening of secrets. So here Christ opens his secrets to us, and we to him. . . .

In friendship, there is mutual solace and comfort one in another. Christ delights himself in his love to the church, and his church delights herself in her love to Christ. . . .

In friendship there is a mutual honor and respect one of another.[7]

Do you see the common strand? Notice the word "mutual" or the phrase "one another" throughout these various facets of Christ's friendship. The point is that he is with us, as one of us, sharing in our life and experience, and the love and comfort that are mutually enjoyed between friends are likewise enjoyed between Christ

6   Sibbes, *Bowels Opened*, 2:37.
7   Sibbes, *Bowels Opened*, 2:37.

and us. In short, he relates to us as a person. Jesus is not the idea of friendship, abstractly; he is an actual friend.

———

It would be cruel to suggest that human friendship is irrelevant once one has been befriended by Christ. God made us for fellowship, for union of heart, with other people. Everyone gets lonely—including introverts.

But Christ's heart for us means that he will be our never-failing friend no matter what friends we do or do not enjoy on earth. He offers us a friendship that gets underneath the pain of our loneliness. While that pain does not go away, its sting is made fully bearable by the far deeper friendship of Jesus. He walks with us through every moment. He knows the pain of being betrayed by a friend, but he will never betray us. He will not even so much as *coolly* welcome us. That is not who he is. That is not his heart.

As his friendship is sweet, so it is constant in all conditions. . . . If other friends fail, as friends may fail, yet this friend will never fail us. If we be not ashamed of him, he will never be ashamed of us. How comfortable would our life be if we could draw out the comfort that this title of *friend* affords! It is a comfortable, a fruitful, an eternal friendship.[8]

---

8   Sibbes, *Bowels Opened*, 2:37. Goodwin has a rich treatment of divine friendship but keeps it at the level of friendship with God, not with Christ specifically, so I have passed over it in this chapter. *Gospel Holiness*, in *Works*, 7:186–213, esp. 7:190–97; cf. 7:240.

13

Why the Spirit?

I will ask the Father, and he will give you another Helper.

JOHN 14:16

THIS IS A BOOK ABOUT CHRIST, the Son, the second person of the Trinity. But we must be careful not to give the impression that what we are seeing in Christ is somehow out of step with the Spirit and the Father. Rather, the Son, "being manifest in the flesh, expresses and utters but what was in the heart of all the three."[1]

So we will give a chapter to each, asking what the Bible teaches about how the heart of Christ relates to the Spirit and then to the Father. We'll take the Spirit in this chapter and the Father in the next.

What is the role of the Holy Spirit? What does he actually do? There are many valid biblical answers to that question. The Spirit:

• Regenerates us (John 3:6–7)
• Convicts us (John 16:8)

---

1   Thomas Goodwin, *A Discourse of Election*, in *The Works of Thomas Goodwin*, 12 vols. (repr., Grand Rapids, MI: Reformation Heritage, 2006), 9:148.

- Empowers us with gifts (1 Cor. 12:4–7)
- Testifies in our hearts that we are God's children (Gal. 4:6)
- Leads us (Gal. 5:18, 25)
- Makes us fruitful (Gal. 5:22–23)
- Grants and nurtures in us resurrection life (Rom. 8:11)
- Enables us to kill sin (Rom. 8:13)
- Intercedes for us when we don't know what to pray (Rom. 8:26–27)
- Guides us into truth (John 16:13)
- Transforms us into the image of Christ (2 Cor. 3:18)

These are all gloriously true. In this chapter I'd like to add just one more to this list: *the Spirit causes us to actually feel Christ's heart for us.*

This overlaps a bit with a few of the operations of the Spirit listed above. But it would be useful to make clear exactly how the Holy Spirit connects to this study of the heart of Jesus. And what I propose in this chapter, once more with help from Thomas Goodwin, is that the Spirit makes the heart of Christ real to us: not just heard, but seen; not just seen, but felt; not just felt, but enjoyed. The Spirit takes what we read in the Bible and believe on paper about Jesus's heart and moves it from theory to reality, from doctrine to experience.

It is one thing, as a child, to be told your father loves you. You believe him. You take him at his word. But it is another thing, unutterably more real, to be swept up in his embrace, to feel the warmth, to hear his beating heart within his chest, to instantly know the protective grip of his arms. It's one thing to hear he loves you; it's another thing to feel his love. This is the glorious work of the Spirit.

In John 14–16 Jesus explains the work of the Spirit as an extension of his own work. And he says that the time in which he himself has left but the Spirit has come is a superior blessing to his people. Notice carefully the flow of thought in John 16 as Jesus makes this point:

> But now I am going to him who sent me, and none of you asks me, "Where are you going?" But because I have said these things to you, sorrow has filled your heart. Nevertheless, I tell you the truth: it is to your advantage that I go away, for if I do not go away, the Helper will not come to you. But if I go, I will send him to you. (John 16:5–7)

What is the advantage of the Spirit coming? The natural reading is that he will rectify something that is wrong. And what is wrong? "Sorrow has filled your heart" (John 16:6). Apparently the coming of the Spirit will do the opposite: fill their hearts with joy. The Spirit replaces sorrow with joy.

The disciples were sorrowful because Jesus was leaving them. He had befriended them and embraced them into his heart, so they thought that Jesus leaving meant Jesus's heart leaving—but the Spirit is the answer to how Jesus can leave them bodily while leaving his heart behind. The Spirit is the continuation of the heart of Christ for his people after the departure of Jesus to heaven.

Reflecting on this passage in John 16, Goodwin presses into the marrow of what Jesus is saying to his disciples: "My father and I have but only one friend, who lies in the bosom of us both, and proceeds from us both, the Holy Ghost, and in the meantime I will send him to you. . . . He shall be a better Comforter unto you than I am to be. . . . He will comfort you better than I should do with my bodily presence." In what way is the Spirit a superior comforter to God's people? "He shall tell you, if you will listen to him, and not grieve him, nothing but stories of my love. . . . All his speech in your hearts will be to advance me, and to greaten my worth and love unto you, and it will be his delight to do it."[2] Goodwin then makes the explicit connection to Christ's heart:

> So that you shall have my heart as surely and as speedily as if I were with you; and he will be continually breaking your hearts, either with my love to you, or yours to me, or both. . . . He will tell you, when I am in heaven, that there is as true a conjunction between me and you, and as true a dearness of affection in me towards you, as is between my Father and me, and that it is as impossible to break this knot, and to take off my heart from you, as my Father's from me.[3]

Have you considered this particular operation of the Holy Spirit? Remember, the Spirit is a person. He can be grieved, for example (Isa. 63:10; Eph. 4:30). What would it look like to treat him as such in our actual lives? What might it look like to open up the vents of our hearts to receive the felt love of Christ as fanned into warm flame by the Holy Spirit? We bear in mind here that the Spirit will never fan the flames of the felt love of Christ beyond the degree to which Christ actually loves us; that is impossible. The Spirit simply causes our apprehension of Christ's heartful love to soar closer to what it actually is. One does not worry that binoculars are going

---

2   Thomas Goodwin, *The Heart of Christ* (Edinburgh: Banner of Truth, 2011), 18–19.
3   Goodwin, *The Heart of Christ*, 19–20.

to make the ballgame look larger than it really is from seats in the upper deck; the binoculars simply make the players appear closer to their actual size.

Jesus said that he is "gentle and lowly in heart" (Matt. 11:29). That is a beautiful statement, and even without the Spirit one could respect and even marvel at it. But the Spirit takes those words of Christ's and interiorizes them at the level of personal individuality. The Spirit turns the recipe into actual taste. That is what Goodwin is saying. All that we see and hear of the gracious heart of Jesus in his earthly life will, during his ascended state, enter into the consciousness of his people as experiential reality. When Paul gets personal in Galatians and speaks of "the Son of God, who loved *me* and gave himself for *me*" (Gal. 2:20), he is saying something that no one could say apart from the Spirit.

This is why, in another place, Paul says that "we have received not the spirit of the world, but the Spirit who is from God, that we might understand the things freely given us by God" (1 Cor. 2:12). To grasp the role of the Holy Spirit, according to this text, we must bear in mind that the Greek word underlying *understood* (*oida*) should not be restricted to merely intellectual apprehension. This verb simply means "to know," and as is generally the case with the Bible's language of epistemology, *knowing* here is something holistic—not less than intellectual apprehension, but more. It is experiential knowing, the way you know the sun is warm when you stand with your face raised to the sky on a cloudless June day. Paul is saying that the Spirit has been given to us in order that we might know, way down deep, the endless grace of the heart of God. "Freely given" in this text is simply the verb form (*charizomai*) of the common Greek word for "grace" (*charis*). The Spirit loves nothing more than to awaken and calm and soothe us with the heart knowledge of what we have been graced with.

The Spirit's role, in summary, is to turn our postcard apprehensions of Christ's great heart of longing affection for us into an experience of sitting on the beach, in a lawn chair, drink in hand, enjoying the actual experience. The Spirit does this decisively, once and for all, at regeneration. But he does it ten thousand times thereafter, as we continue through sin, folly, or boredom to drift from the felt experience of his heart.

14

Father of Mercies

. . . the Father of mercies and God of all comfort.

2 CORINTHIANS 1:3

"WHAT COMES INTO OUR MINDS when we think about God is the most important thing about us." So begins A. W. Tozer's book *The Knowledge of the Holy.*[1] One way to understand the purpose of this study of Christ's heart is that it is an attempt to make our mental image of who God is more accurate. I am seeking to help us leave behind our natural, fallen intuitions that God is distant and parsimonious and to step into the liberating realization that he is gentle and lowly in heart.

But our study focuses on the Son of God. What about the Father? To pick up Tozer's statement, should we envision the Son as gentle and lowly but the Father as something else? This chapter answers that question.

---

1   A. W. Tozer, *The Knowledge of the Holy* (New York: HarperCollins, 1961), 1.

Classic, mainstream, Protestant atonement theology has always understood that the justice of God was vindicated and the wrath of God was satisfied in the work of the Son. Christ did not live, die, and rise from the dead as a moral example mainly or a triumph over Satan mainly or a demonstration of his love mainly. Supremely, the work of the Son, and especially his death and resurrection, satisfied the Father's righteous wrath against the horror of human rebellion against him. His wrath was propitiated—turned away, assuaged.

This is not to suggest that the Father's disposition toward his people is different from that of his Son. A common perception among Christians is that, yes, to some degree anyway, the Father is less inclined to love and forgive than the Son.

This is not what the Bible teaches.

How then do we understand the fact that the Father had wrath that needed to be satisfied, and the Son was the one who did the work needed to provide that satisfaction? Surely this suggests a different posture toward us from the Father and from the Son?

The key is to understand that at the level of legal acquittal, the Father's wrath had to be assuaged in order for sinners to be brought back into his favor, but at the level of his own internal desire and affection, he was as eager as the Son for this atonement to take place. Objectively, the Father was the one needing to be placated; subjectively, his heart was one with the Son. We err when we draw conclusions about who he is *subjectively* based on what needed to happen *objectively*. The Puritans would often speak of the Father and Son agreeing in eternity past, both of them together, to redeem a sinful people. Theologians call this the *pactum salutis*, the "covenant of redemption," referring to what the triune God agreed upon before the creation of the world. The Father did not need more persuading than the Son. On the contrary, his ordaining of the way of redemption reflects the same heart of love that the Son's accomplishing of redemption does.[2]

In later chapters we will see the Old Testament speak of God in ways that are consonant with Jesus's statement in the New Testament that he is "gentle and lowly in heart." For now we consider what the New Testament says about the Father. We take as our focal text 2 Corinthians 1:3, where the apostle Paul starts off the body of a letter with the following words of worship:

> Blessed be the God and Father of our Lord Jesus Christ, the Father of mercies and God of all comfort.

"The Father of mercies." As Paul opens 2 Corinthians he gives us a window into what came into *his* mind when he thought about God.

Yes, the Father is just and righteous. Unswervingly, unendingly. Without such a doctrine, such a reassurance, we would have no hope that all wrongs would one day be righted. But what is his heart? What flows out from his deepest being? What does he beget? Mercies.

He is the Father of mercies. Just as a father begets children who reflect who he is, the divine Father begets mercies that reflect him. There is a family resemblance between the Father and mercy. He is "more the Father of mercies than Satan is said to be the father of sin."[3]

---

2 See, e.g., Flavel's moving speculation of a "conversation" between the Father and the Son to save sinners, in *The Works of John Flavel*, 6 vols. (Edinburgh: Banner of Truth, 1968), 1:61. I am grateful to my dad, Ray Ortlund, for drawing my attention to this passage in Flavel. See also Goodwin's work *Man's Restoration by Grace*, a short book outlining the Trinity's distinct roles in, yet mutual agreement on, the work of redemption. Thomas Goodwin, *The Works of Thomas Goodwin*, 12 vols. (repr., Grand Rapids, MI: Reformation Heritage, 2006), 7:519–41.
3 Goodwin, *Works*, 2:179.

The word "mercies" (*oikteirmon*) occurs only five times in the New Testament. One of these is James 5:11, where it is put in synonymous parallelism with divine compassion: "You have heard of the steadfastness of Job, and you have seen the purpose of the Lord, how the Lord is compassionate (*polusplanchnos*) and merciful (*oikteirmon*)." We noted in chapter 11 that the word for Jesus's deepest compassion is *splanchnizo*, and you can see that same word root in what is translated in James 5:11 as "compassionate." Here, though, the word is even richer; it has a prefix (*polu-*) meaning "much" or "greatly." The Lord, according to James 5:11, is "much compassionate." And that the Lord is much compassionate or greatly compassioned is synonymous with saying that he is merciful.

To speak of God the Father as "the Father of mercies" is to say that he is the one who multiplies compassionate mercies to his needful, wayward, messy, fallen, wandering people. Speaking of Christ's love for his people, Goodwin makes a seamless move from speaking of the Son's heart to speaking of the Father's heart.

> His love is not a forced love, which he strives only to bear toward us, because his Father hath commanded him to marry us; but it is his nature, his disposition. . . . This disposition is free and natural to him; he should not be God's Son else, nor take after his heavenly Father, unto whom it is natural to show mercy, but not so to punish, which is his strange work, but mercy pleases him; he is "the Father of mercies," he begets them naturally.[4]

We'll return in the next chapter to what it means that mercy is God's "natural" work and punishment his "strange" work. For now, just notice

4   Thomas Goodwin, *The Heart of Christ* (Edinburgh: Banner of Truth, 2011), 60.

the way Goodwin helps us to see that the label "Father of mercies" is the Bible's way of taking us into the deepest recesses of who God the Father is. A correct understanding of the triune God is not that of a Father whose central disposition is judgment and a Son whose central disposition is love. The heart of both is one and the same; this is, after all, one God, not two. Theirs is a heart of redeeming love, not compromising justice and wrath but beautifully satisfying justice and wrath.

In another place Goodwin reflects on the mercy of God the Father. It is a fitting meditation on 2 Corinthians 1:3.

> God has a multitude of all kinds of mercies. As our hearts and the devil are the father of variety of sins, so God is the father of variety of mercies. There is no sin or misery but God has a mercy for it. He has a multitude of mercies of every kind.
>
> As there are variety of miseries which the creature is subject unto, so he has in himself a shop, a treasury of all sorts of mercies, divided into several promises in the Scripture, which are but as so many boxes of this treasure, the caskets of variety of mercies.
>
> If your heart be hard, his mercies are tender.
>
> If your heart be dead, he has mercy to liven it.
>
> If you be sick, he has mercy to heal you.
>
> If you be sinful, he has mercies to sanctify and cleanse you.
>
> As large and as various as are our wants, so large and various are his mercies. So we may come boldly to find grace and mercy to help us in time of need, a mercy for every need. All the mercies that are in his own heart he has transplanted into several beds in the garden of the promises, where they grow, and

he has abundance of variety of them, suited to all the variety of the diseases of the soul.[5]

———

What should come into our mind when we think about God? The triune God is three in one, a fountain of endless mercies extending to, meeting, and overflowingly providing for us in all our many needs and failures and wanderings. This is who he is, Father no less than Son, Son no less than Father.

Beyond what we are conscious of at any given moment, the Father's tender care envelopes us with pursuing gentleness, sweetly governing every last detail of our lives. He sovereignly ordains the particular angle of the flutter of the leaf that falls from the tree and the breeze that knocked it free (Matt. 10:29–31), and he sovereignly ordains the bomb that evil minds detonate (Amos 3:6; Luke 13:1–5). But through and underneath and fueling all that washes into our lives, great and small, is the heart of a Father.

Who is God the Father? Just that: our Father. Some of us had great dads growing up. Others of us were horribly mistreated or abandoned by them. Whatever the case, the good in our earthly dads is a faint pointer to the true goodness of our heavenly Father, and the bad in our earthly dads is the photo negative of who our heavenly Father is. He is the Father of whom every human father is a shadow (Eph. 3:15).

In John 14, Philip asks Jesus to show the disciples the Father (John 14:8). Jesus responds: "Have I been with you so long, and you still do not know me, Philip? Whoever has seen me has seen the

———

5 Goodwin, *Works*, 2:187–88. Cf. Goodwin, *Works*, 2:180, also citing 2 Cor. 1:3: "He is the spring of all mercy, so it is natural to him, as it is to a father to beget children."

Father. How can you say, 'Show us the Father'? Do you not believe that I am in the Father and the Father is in me?" (John 14:9–10).

"Whoever has seen me has seen the Father."

Elsewhere the New Testament calls Christ "the radiance of the glory of God and the exact imprint of his nature" (Heb. 1:3). Jesus is the embodiment of who God is. He is the tangible epitomization of God. Jesus Christ is the visible manifestation of the invisible God (2 Cor. 4:4, 6). In him we see heaven's eternal heart walking around on two legs in time and space. When we see the heart of Christ, then, throughout the four Gospels, we are seeing the very compassion and tenderness of who God himself most deeply is.

As you consider the Father's heart for you, remember that he is the Father of mercies. He is not cautious in his tenderness toward you. He multiplies mercies matched to your every need, and there is nothing he would rather do. "Remember," said the Puritan John Flavel, "that this God in whose hand are all creatures, is your Father, and is much more tender of you than you are, or can be, of yourself."[6] Your gentlest treatment of yourself is less gentle than the way your heavenly Father handles you. His tenderness toward you outstrips what you are even capable of toward yourself.

The heart of Christ is gentle and lowly. And that is the perfect picture of who the Father is. "The Father himself loves you" (John 16:27).

---

6   John Flavel, *Keeping the Heart: How to Maintain Your Love for God* (Fearn, Scotland: Christian Heritage, 2012), 57.

15

His "Natural" Work and
His "Strange" Work

He does not afflict from his heart.

LAMENTATIONS 3:33

AT THIS POINT, we turn to the Old Testament. We have been considering the heart of Christ, and even of the Father, from the New Testament. How does this fit with the Old Testament?

After spending a handful of chapters in the Old Testament, we'll conclude our study by returning to the New Testament for the final few chapters.

What I want to demonstrate in this chapter and the next three is that when we see Christ unveil his deepest heart as gentle and lowly, he is continuing on the natural trajectory of what God had already been revealing about himself throughout the Old Testament. Jesus provides new sharpness to who God is, but not fundamentally new content. The Gospels themselves show that they understood the Old Testament to be preparing us for a "humble" Savior (Matt. 21:5).[1] The incarnate Son does not send our understanding of who God is spinning off in a new direction. He simply provides in unprecedented flesh-and-blood reality what God had already been trying to convince his people of down through the centuries. As Calvin put it, the Old Testament is the shadowy revelation of God—true but dim. The New Testament is the substance.[2]

A good launching off point as we consider the heart of God in the Old Testament is Lamentations 3.

———

No book in the Bible is so striking in its joining of profound emotion with literary intricacy as Lamentations. The author (perhaps Jeremiah) is pouring his heart out, lamenting the destruction of Jerusalem in 587 BC by the Babylonians and the horrors of starvation, death, and hopelessness that ensued. Yet he pours out his heart through a series of five ornately structured poems reflecting extreme literary care. You can see this by simply looking at the versification in your English Bible. Although the chapters and verse numbers were not added until many centuries after Lamentations was written, these divisions in our modern Bibles do reflect the clear divisions of the book itself. You'll notice that of the five chapters, the first two and the last two each have twenty-two verses. The middle chapter, chapter 3, has

1   The Greek word for "humble" in Matt. 21:5, quoting the prophecy from Zech. 9:9 that "your king is coming to you; . . . *humble* and mounted on a donkey," is the same one (*praus*) used in Matt. 11:29 when Jesus calls himself "gentle."
2   John Calvin, *Institutes of the Christian Religion*, ed. John T. McNeill, trans. Ford L. Battles, 2 vols. (Louisville, KY: Westminster John Knox, 1960), 2.11.1–12.

three times that many—sixty-six. Each chapter is itself a carefully constructed lament.

With this overarching structure to the book in view, we understand that the literary high point to the letter is verse 33 of chapter 3. It is the exact middle of the book and captures the heart of the book. Lamentations 3:33 is the book of Lamentations in a nutshell.

What does it say? It grounds the surrounding assurances of God's eventual mercy and restoration with the following theology:

> For he does not afflict from his heart
>   or grieve the children of men.

There is an implicit premise in this verse and an explicit statement. The implicit premise is that God is indeed the one who afflicts. The explicit statement is that he does not do it from his heart.

The implicit premise must be fully embraced before moving on to the explicit statement. When we speak of what God does or does not do from his heart, we are not limiting his sovereign rule more broadly; indeed, to the degree that we believe God is sovereign in all our affliction, to that degree we are able to be comforted that he does not afflict us from his heart.

First, then, we remember the beauty of utter divine sovereignty over all things, good *and bad*. The stubbed toe, the poison ivy, the backstabbing friend, the chronic neck pain, the people-pleasing boss who won't stand up for us, the wayward child, the vomiting at 2:00 a.m., the unrelenting darkness of depression. The Belgic Confession beautifully articulates God's governance of all things in its teaching on divine providence, part of which reads:

This doctrine gives us unspeakable comfort since it teaches us that nothing can happen to us by chance but only by the arrangement of our gracious heavenly Father, who watches over us with fatherly care, sustaining all creatures under his lordship, so that not one of the hairs on our heads (for they are all numbered) nor even a little bird can fall to the ground without the will of our Father. (Art. 13)

Throughout Lamentations this unfiltered view of divine sovereignty is everywhere at play. Glancing at chapter 3, for example, we see verse after verse beginning with "He," as the author recounts all the horrors that God himself has brought upon Israel (3:2–16). But at the theological bull's-eye of the whole book, we are told that God does not bring such pain "from his heart."

———

Here in Lamentations, the Bible is taking us deep into God himself. The one who rules and ordains all things brings affliction into our lives with a certain divine reluctance. He is not reluctant about the ultimate good that is going to be brought about through that pain; that indeed is why he is doing it. But something recoils within him in sending that affliction. The pain itself does not reflect his heart. He is not a platonic force pulling heaven's levers and pulleys in a way that is detached from the real pain and anguish we feel at his hand. He is—if I can put it this way without questioning his divine perfections—conflicted within himself when he sends affliction into our lives. God is indeed punishing Israel for their waywardness as the Babylonians sweep through the city. He is sending what they deserve. But his deepest heart is their merciful restoration.

Goodwin explains:

My brethren, though God is just, yet his mercy may in some respect said to be more natural to him than all acts of justice itself that God does show, I mean vindictive justice. In these acts of justice there is a satisfaction to an attribute, in that he meets and is even with sinners. Yet there is a kind of violence done to himself in it, the Scripture so expresses it; there is something in it that is contrary to him. "I desire not the death of a sinner"—that is, I delight not simply in it, for pleasure's sake. . . . When he exercises acts of justice, it is for a higher end, it is not simply for the thing itself. There is always something in his heart against it.

But when he comes to show mercy, to manifest that it is his nature and disposition, it is said that he does it with his whole heart. There is nothing at all in him that is against it. The act itself pleases him for itself. There is no reluctance in him.

Therefore in Lamentations 3:33, when he speaks of punishing, he says, "He does not from his heart afflict nor grieve the children of men." But when he comes to speak of showing mercy, he says he does it "with his whole heart, and with his whole soul," as the expression is in Jeremiah 32:41. And therefore acts of justice are called his "strange work" and his "strange act" in Isaiah 28:21. But when he comes to show mercy, he rejoices over them, to do them good, with his whole heart and with his whole soul.[3]

Goodwin brings in a few other texts here—Jeremiah 32:41, where God says of his restoring work that "I will rejoice in doing them good, and I will plant them in this land in faithfulness, with all my heart and all my soul"; and Isaiah 28:21, where God's judging activity is

---

3   Thomas Goodwin, *The Works of Thomas Goodwin*, 12 vols. (repr., Grand Rapids, MI: Reformation Heritage, 2006), 2:179–80.

called his "strange" and "alien" work. Tying these texts in with Lamentations 3:33, Goodwin is drawing out the Bible's revelation of what God's deepest heart is—that is, what he delights to do, what is most natural to him. Mercy is natural to him. Punishment is unnatural.

Some of us view God's heart as brittle, easily offended. Some of us view his heart as cold, uneasily moved. The Old Testament gives us a God whose heart defies these innate human expectations of who he is.

We must tread cautiously here. All of God's attributes are nonnegotiable. For God to cease to be, say, just would un-God him just as much as if he were to cease to be good. Theologians speak of God's simplicity, by which we mean that God is not the sum total of a number of attributes, like pieces of a pie making a whole pie; rather, God is every attribute perfectly. God does not have parts. He is just. He is wrathful. He is good. And so on, each in endless perfection.

Even when it comes to the matter of God's own heart, we see complexity in the opening pages of Scripture. The first two major decisions God makes following creation are both said to be matters of his heart: destroying all flesh except Noah (6:6), and accepting Noah's sacrifice and determining never to flood the earth again (8:21). Apparently God is also complex enough to make decisions both of judgment and of mercy out of his heart.

Yet at the same time, if we are to follow closely and yield fully to Scripture's testimony, we are walked into the breathtaking claim that from another, deeper angle, there are some things that pour out of God more naturally than others. God is unswervingly just. But what is his disposition? What is he on the edge of his seat eager to do? If you catch me off guard, what will leap out of me before I have time to regain composure will likely be grouchiness. If you catch God off guard, what leaps out most freely is blessing. The impulse to do good. The desire to swallow us up in joy.[4] This is why Goodwin can say of God that "all his attributes seem but to set out his love."[5]

Another key Old Testament text is Hosea 11, where, on the heels of Israel's spiritual fornication and abandoning of her divine lover, God recounts with stirring terms of affection how he has felt toward Israel: "When Israel was a child, I loved him" (Hos. 11:1), and indeed "it was I who taught Ephraim to walk; I took them up by their arms. . . . I led them with cords of kindness, with the bands of love . . . and I bent down to them and fed them" (11:3–4). Yet despite this tender care, "My people are bent on turning away from me" (11:7) and persist in idolatry (11:2).

What then is God's response?

How can I give you up, O Ephraim?
How can I hand you over, O Israel?
How can I make you like Admah?
How can I treat you like Zeboiim?
My heart recoils within me;
my compassion grows warm and tender.
I will not execute my burning anger;
I will not again destroy Ephraim;
for I am God and not a man,
the Holy One in your midst,
and I will not come in wrath. (Hos. 11:8–9)

---

4 A particularly helpful explanation of divine simplicity is Herman Bavinck, *Reformed Dogmatics*, ed. John Bolt, trans. John Vriend, 4 vols. (Grand Rapids, MI: Baker, 2003–2008), 2:173–77, who sees God's simplicity as entailing necessarily that he is "the highest love" (2:176).

5 Goodwin, *Of Gospel Holiness in the Heart and Life*, in *Works*, 7:211.

We considered this text in chapter 7. I draw it to mind here not only because it uniquely tunnels into the heart of God in a way similar to Lamentations 3 but also because, in commenting on Hosea 11:8, Jonathan Edwards says something strikingly similar to what Goodwin says above on Lamentations 3. "God has no pleasure in the destruction or calamity of persons or people," writes Edwards. "He had rather they should turn and continue in peace. He is well-pleased if they forsake their evil ways, that he may not have occasion to execute his wrath upon them. He is a God that delights in mercy, and judgment is his strange work."[6]

Following the lead of Scripture, both Edwards and Goodwin call mercy what God most deeply delights in and judgment his "strange work."

———

As we read and reflect on this teaching from great theologians of the past such as Jonathan Edwards or Thomas Goodwin, we need to understand that they are not calling judgment God's "strange" work out of a diluted sense of the wrath and justice of God.

Edwards is most famous for his sermon "Sinners in the Hands of an Angry God," a terrifying depiction of the precarious state of the impenitent under the wrath of God—though not so terrifying

---

6 Jonathan Edwards, "Impending Judgments Averted Only by Reformation," in *The Works of Jonathan Edwards*, vol. 14, *Sermons and Discourses, 1723–1729*, ed. Kenneth P. Minkema (New Haven, CT: Yale University Press, 1997), 221. Similarly miscellany 1081 in *The Works of Jonathan Edwards*, vol. 20, *The "Miscellanies," 833–1152*, ed. Amy Plantinga Pauw (New Haven, CT: Yale University Press, 2002), 464–65.

as some other sermons of his, such as "The Justice of God in the Damnation of Sinners." *This* was the man who affirmed that God "delights in mercy, but judgment is his strange work."

As for Goodwin, he stood up and spoke from the floor more often (357 times) than any other divine at the creation of the Westminster standards in England in the 1640s—that great, precise, hell-believing, wrath-affirming statement of faith that teaches that when those out of Christ die now, they "are cast into hell, where they remain in torments and utter darkness, reserved to the judgment of the great day" (Westminster Confession of Faith 32.1); and at the final judgment, "the wicked who know not God, and obey not the gospel of Jesus Christ, shall be cast into eternal torments, and be punished with everlasting destruction from the presence of the Lord" (33.2). That was Goodwin's theology; he had as influential a hand as any in crafting it. As for Goodwin's own writing, he had no hesitation writing of "the most exquisite pains" of hell, where "God's wrath and his word do torment men forever," for he "knows how to torture exquisitely" those who persist in sin and do not repent.[7]

Edwards, Goodwin, and the theological river in which they stand were not mushy. They affirmed and preached and taught divine wrath and an eternal hell. They saw these doctrines in the Bible (2 Thess. 1:5–12, to cite just one text). But because they knew their Bibles inside and out and followed their Bibles scrupulously, they discerned also a strand of teaching in Scripture about who God most deeply is—about his heart.

---

7   Goodwin, *Works*, 7:304, 305.

And this, perhaps, is the secret to their time-tested influence. There is a kind of preaching and Bible teaching that has not felt the heart of God for his fickle people, has not tasted what naturally pours forth from him, which for all its precision ultimately deadens its hearers. Not so the Puritans or the great preachers of the Great Awakening. They knew that when God deigns to lavish goodness on his people, he does it with a certain naturalness reflective of the depths of who he is. For God to be merciful is for God to be God.

Left to our own natural intuitions about God, we will conclude that mercy is his strange work and judgment his natural work. Rewiring our vision of God as we study the Scripture, we see, helped by the great teachers of the past, that judgment is his strange work and mercy his natural work.

He does afflict and grieve the children of men. But not from his heart.

16

The Lord, the Lord

"A God merciful and gracious, slow to anger . . ."

EXODUS 34:6

WHO IS GOD?

If we could pick only one passage from the Old Testament to answer that question, it would be hard to improve upon Exodus 34. God is revealing himself to Moses, causing his glory to pass by Moses, whom God has put in a cleft in the rock (33:22). At the critical moment we read:

> The LORD passed before him and proclaimed, "The LORD, the LORD, a God merciful and gracious, slow to anger, and abounding in steadfast love and faithfulness, keeping steadfast love for thousands, forgiving iniquity and transgression and sin, but who will by no means clear the guilty, visiting the iniquity of the fathers on the children and the children's children, to the third and the fourth generation." (Ex. 34:6–7)

Short of the incarnation itself, this is perhaps the high point of divine revelation in all the Bible. One objective way to demonstrate that point is how often this text is picked up elsewhere in the Old Testament. Time and again the prophets who followed Moses draw on these two verses from Exodus to affirm who God is. One of these occurs in the immediate context of the verse we have just considered, Lamentations 3:33. In the previous verse of that passage, God is described as having "compassion according to the abundance of his steadfast love" (3:32), and the author uses several of the key Hebrew words underlying the revelation of Exodus 34:6–7. Many other texts likewise echo Exodus 34, including Numbers 14:18; Nehemiah 9:17; 13:22; Psalms 5:8; 69:14; 86:5, 15; 103:8; 145:8; Isaiah 63:7; Joel 2:13; Jonah 4:2; and Nahum 1:3.

Exodus 34:6–7 is not a one-off descriptor, a peripheral passing comment. In this text we climb into the very center of who God is. Old Testament scholar Walter Brueggemann gives this text special attention in his *Theology of the Old Testament*, calling it "an exceedingly important, stylized, quite self-conscious characterization of Yahweh, a formulation so studied that it may be reckoned to be something of a classic normative statement to which Israel regularly returned, meriting the label 'credo.'"[1]

What then is Israel's "credo" about who God is?

Not what we would expect.

———

1   Walter Brueggemann, *Theology of the Old Testament: Testimony, Dispute, Advocacy* (Minneapolis: Fortress, 1997), 216.

What do you think of when you hear the phrase "the glory of God"? Do you picture the immense size of the universe? A thundering, terrifying voice from the clouds?

In Exodus 33 Moses asks God, "Please show me your glory" (33:18). How does God respond? "I will make all my goodness pass before you" (33:19). Goodness? Isn't the glory of God a matter of his greatness, not his goodness? Apparently not. God then goes on to speak of showing mercy and grace to whomever he wills (33:19). He then tells Moses that he will place him in the cleft of the rock and that (once again) his *glory* will pass by (33:22). And the Lord does pass by and yet (once again) defines his glory in 34:6–7 as a matter of mercy and grace:

> . . . merciful and gracious, slow to anger, and abounding in steadfast love and faithfulness, keeping steadfast love for thousands, forgiving iniquity and transgression and sin, but who will by no means clear the guilty, visiting the iniquity of the fathers on the children and the children's children, to the third and the fourth generation.

When we speak of God's glory, we are speaking of who God is, what he is like, his distinctive resplendence, what makes God *God*. And when God himself sets the terms on what his glory is, he surprises us into wonder. Our deepest instincts expect him to be thundering, gavel swinging, judgment relishing. We expect the bent of God's heart to be retribution to our waywardness. And then Exodus 34 taps us on the shoulder and stops us in our tracks. The bent of God's heart is mercy. His glory is his goodness. His glory is his lowliness. "Great is the glory of the LORD. For though the LORD is high, he regards the lowly" (Ps. 138:5–6).

Consider the words of Exodus 34:6–7.

"Merciful and gracious." These are the first words out of God's own mouth after proclaiming his name ("the LORD," or "I am"). *The first words.* The only two words Jesus will use to describe his own heart are *gentle* and *lowly* (Matt. 11:29). And the first two words God uses to describe who he is are *merciful* and *gracious.* God does not reveal his glory as, "The LORD, the LORD, exacting and precise," or, "The LORD, the LORD, tolerant and overlooking," or, "The LORD, the LORD, disappointed and frustrated." His highest priority and deepest delight and first reaction—his heart—is merciful and gracious. He gently accommodates himself to our terms rather than overwhelming us with his.

"Slow to anger." The Hebrew phrase is literally "long of nostrils." Picture an angry bull, pawing the ground, breathing loudly, nostrils flared. That would be, so to speak, "short-nosed." But the Lord is long-nosed. He doesn't have his finger on the trigger. It takes much accumulated provoking to draw out his ire. Unlike us, who are often emotional dams ready to break, God can put up with a lot. This is why the Old Testament speaks of God being "provoked to anger" by his people dozens of times (especially in Deuteronomy; 1–2 Kings; and Jeremiah). But not once are we told that God is "provoked to love" or "provoked to mercy." His anger requires provocation; his mercy is pent up, ready to gush forth. We tend to think: divine anger is pent up, spring-loaded; divine mercy is slow to build. It's just the opposite. Divine mercy is ready to burst forth at the slightest prick.[2] (For fallen humans, we learn in the New Testament, this is reversed. We are to provoke one another to love, according to Hebrews 10:24.

2   I am grateful to Wade Urig for helping me see this.

Yahweh needs no provoking to love, only to anger. We need no provoking to anger, only to love. Once again, the Bible is one long attempt to deconstruct our natural vision of who God actually is.)

"Abounding in steadfast love and faithfulness." This is covenant language. There is one Hebrew word underlying the English phrase "steadfast love." It is the word *hesed*, which refers to God's special commitment to the people with whom he has gladly bound himself in an unbreakable covenant bond. The word "faithfulness" gets at this too—he will never throw his hands up in the air, despite all the reasons his people give him to do so. He refuses even to entertain the notion of forsaking us who deserve to be, or of withdrawing his heart from us the way we do toward others who hurt us. Therefore he is not simply *existing* in large-hearted covenant commitment but *abounding* in it. His determined commitment to us never runs dry.

"Keeping steadfast love for thousands." This could equally be translated "keeping steadfast love to a thousand generations," as is explicitly stated in Deuteronomy 7:9: "Know therefore that the LORD your God is God, the faithful God who keeps covenant and steadfast love with those who love him and keep his commandments, to a thousand generations." This does not mean that his goodness shuts off with generation number 1,001. It is God's own way of saying: *There is no termination date on my commitment to you. You can't get rid of my grace to you. You can't outrun my mercy. You can't evade my goodness. My heart is set on you.*

"Visiting the iniquity of the fathers on the children and the children's children, to the third and fourth generation." This closing element, though initially hard to hear, is vital—and, on reflection, fosters further comfort. Without it, all that has come before might be misunderstood as mere leniency. But God is not a softie. He is the one perfectly fair person in the universe. God is not mocked; we reap what we sow (Gal. 6:7). Sin and guilt pass down from generation to generation. We see this all around us in the world. But notice what God says. His covenant love flows down to a thousand generations; but he visits generational sins to the third or fourth generation. Do you see the difference? Yes, our sins will be passed down to our children and grandchildren. But God's goodness will be passed down in a way that inexorably swallows up all our sins. His mercies travel down a thousand generations, far eclipsing the third or fourth generation.

———

That is who God is. That, according to his own testimony, is his heart.

The asymmetry of Exodus 34:6–7 startles us. Mercy and love loom large; retributive justice is acknowledged but almost as a necessary afterthought. John Owen put it this way in commenting on this passage:

> When [God] solemnly declared his nature by his name to the full, that we might know and fear him, he does it by an enumeration of those properties which may convince us of his compassionateness and forbearance, and not till the close of all makes any mention of his severity, as that which he will not exercise towards any but such as by whom his compassion is despised.[3]

The Puritans understood that in this revelation to Moses, God is opening up to us his deepest heart. In the supreme revelation of

3   John Owen, *An Exposition of the Epistle to the Hebrews*, in W. H. Goold, ed., *The Works of John Owen*, vol. 25 (repr., Edinburgh: Banner of Truth, 1965), 483.

God in all the Old Testament, God himself does not feel a need to balance out communications of mercy with immediate and equal communications of his wrath. Rather he speaks of himself, as Richard Sibbes put it, "clothed all in sweet attributes." Sibbes goes on to say: "If we would know the name of God, and see God as he is pleased and delighted to discover himself to us, let us know him by those names that he proclaims there, showing that the glory of the Lord in the gospel especially shines in mercy."[4]

What we see in Exodus 34, and what Owen and Sibbes confirm, echoes throughout the rest of the Bible, such as at Isaiah 54:7–8, where the Lord says:

> For a brief moment I deserted you,
>   but with great compassion I will gather you.
> In overflowing anger for a moment
>   I hid my face from you,
> but with everlasting love I will have compassion on you.

The Christian life, from one angle, is the long journey of letting our natural assumption about who God is, over many decades, fall away, being slowly replaced with God's own insistence on who he is. This is hard work. It takes a lot of sermons and a lot of suffering to believe that God's deepest heart is "merciful and gracious, slow to anger." The fall in Genesis 3 not only sent us into condemnation and exile. The fall also entrenched in our minds dark thoughts of God, thoughts that are only dug out over multiple exposures to the gospel over many years. Perhaps Satan's greatest victory in your life

4   Richard Sibbes, *The Excellency of the Gospel Above the Law*, in *The Works of Richard Sibbes*, ed. A. B. Grosart, 7 vols. (Edinburgh: Banner of Truth, 1983), 4:245.

today is not the sin in which you regularly indulge but the dark thoughts of God's heart that cause you to go there in the first place and keep you cool toward him in the wake of it.

But of course the final proof of who God is cannot be found in Exodus but in Matthew, Mark, Luke, and John. In Exodus 33–34 Moses cannot see God's face and live, because it would incinerate him. But what if one day humans did see the face of God in a way that did not incinerate them? When John speaks of the Word becoming flesh he says, "We have seen his glory"—we have seen what Moses asked to see but couldn't—"full of grace and truth" (John 1:14, identifying Christ as possessing in fullness the same traits as God in Ex. 34:6).

John is not the only Gospel writer to draw connections back to Exodus 33–34. Consider this: the revelation of Exodus 34 follows a miraculous feeding (Ex. 16:1–36) and discussion of the sabbath (31:12–18); involves God's representative leader talking with God on a mountain (32:1, 15, 19; 34:2, 3, 29); concludes with God's people as terrified of, calmed by, drawing near to, and speaking with God's representative leader as this leader comes down from a mountain (34:30–31); is immediately followed by a recounting of marveling among the people as the object of their worship goes in the midst of the people (34:9–10); and is then followed thereafter by a further meeting between God's representative leader and God, resulting in the leader's face shining radiantly (34:29–33).

Every one of these narratival details occurs in Mark 6:45–52 and its surrounding context, as Jesus walks on the water.[5]

---

5   That is: a miraculous feeding (Mark 6:30–44); discussion of the Sabbath (6:2); God's representative leader talking with God on a mountain (6:46); concluding with God's people terrified of, calmed by, drawing near to, and speaking with God's representative leader as this leader

THE LORD, THE LORD

And now we begin to see why Jesus intended to "pass by" his disciples, struggling at the oars on the Sea of Galilee. The text says that "he saw that they were making headway painfully, for the wind was against them. And about the fourth watch of the night he came to them, walking on the sea. He meant to pass by them" (Mark 6:48). Why would he intend to pass by them? The reason is that Jesus does not merely intend to "pass by" the disciples the way one car on the highway may bypass others. His passing by is far more significant and only understood against its Old Testament background. Four times in Exodus 33–34 the Lord says he will "pass by" Moses, the Septuagint (the Greek Old Testament) using the same word (*parerchomai*) that Mark uses.

The Lord passed by Moses and revealed that his deepest glory is seen in his mercy and grace. Jesus came to do in flesh and blood what God had done only in wind and voice in the Old Testament.

When we see the Lord revealing his truest character to Moses in Exodus 34, we are seeing the shadow that will one day yield to the shadow caster, Jesus Christ, in the Gospels. We are being given in 2-D what will explode into our own space-and-time continuum in 3-D centuries later, at the height of all of human history.

We are being told of God's deepest heart in Exodus 34. But we are shown that heart in the Galilean carpenter, who testified that this was his heart throughout his life and then proved it when he went to a Roman cross, descending into the hell of God-forsakenness in our place.

---

comes down a mountain (6:49–50); is immediately followed by a recounting of marveling among the people as Jesus in the midst of the people (6:53–56); and is followed thereafter by a further meeting between God's representative leader and God, resulting in the leader's face shining radiantly (9:2–13). Readers who wish to see these connections laid out at length may consult Dane Ortlund, "The Old Testament Background and Eschatological Significance of Jesus Walking on the Sea (Mark 6:45–52)," *Neotestamentica* 46 (2012): 319–37.

17

His Ways Are Not Our Ways

My thoughts are not your thoughts.
ISAIAH 55:8

THE MESSAGE OF THIS BOOK is that we tend to project our natural expectations about who God is onto him instead of fighting to let the Bible surprise us into what God himself says. Perhaps nowhere in the Bible is that point made more clearly than in Isaiah 55. "There is nothing that troubles our consciences more," said John Calvin on this passage, "than when we think that God is like ourselves."[1]

When life takes a difficult turn, Christians often remind others, with a shrug, "His ways are not our ways"—communicating the mysteries of divine providence by which he orchestrates events in ways that surprise us. The mysterious depth of divine providence is, of course, a precious biblical truth. But the passage in which we find "his ways are not our ways" comes from Isaiah 55. And in

---

1   John Calvin, *Commentary on the Prophet Isaiah*, vol. 4, trans. William Pringle (repr., Grand Rapids, MI: Baker, 2003), 169.

155

context, it means something quite different. It is a statement not of the surprise of God's mysterious providence but of the surprise of God's compassionate heart. The full passage goes like this:

> Seek the LORD while he may be found;
>   call upon him while he is near;
> let the wicked forsake his way,
>   and the unrighteous man his thoughts;
> Let him return to the LORD, that he may have compassion
>   on him,
>   and to our God, for he will abundantly pardon.
> For my thoughts are not your thoughts,
>   neither are your ways my ways, declares the LORD.
> For as high as the heavens are above the earth,
>   so are my ways higher than your ways
>   and my thoughts than your thoughts. (Isa. 55:6–9)

The first part of this passage tells us what to do. The second part tells us why. The transition comes toward the end of verse 7 (which concludes, "for he will abundantly pardon"). But notice the exact line of reasoning.

God calls us to seek him, to call on him, and invites even the wicked to return to the Lord. What will happen when we do this? God will "have compassion on" us (v. 7). The parallelism of Hebrew poetry then gives us another way of saying that God will exercise compassion toward us: "He will abundantly pardon" (v. 7). This is profound consolation for us as we find ourselves time and again wandering away from the Father, looking for soul calm anywhere but in his embrace and instruction. Returning to God in fresh contrition, however ashamed and disgusted with ourselves, he will not tepidly pardon. He will abundantly pardon. He does not merely accept us. He sweeps us up in his arms again.

But notice what the text then does. Verses 8 and 9 take us deeper into this compassion and abundant pardon. Verse 7 has told us what God does; verses 8 and 9 tell us who he is. Or to put it differently, God knows that *even when we hear of his compassionate pardon, we latch on to that promise with a diminished view of the heart from which that compassionate pardon flows.* This is why the Lord continues:

> For my thoughts are not your thoughts,
>> neither are your ways my ways, declares the LORD.
> For as high as the heavens are above the earth,
>> so are my ways higher than your ways
>> and my thoughts than your thoughts.

What is God saying? He is telling us that we cannot view his expressions of his mercy with our old eyes. Our very view of God must change. What would we say to a seven-year-old who, upon being given a birthday gift by his loving father, immediately scrambled to reach for his piggy bank to try to pay his dad back? How painful to a father's heart. That child needs to change his very view of who his father is and what his father delights to do.

The natural flow of the fallen human heart is toward reciprocity, tit-for-tat payback, equanimity, balancing of the scales. We are far more intractably *law-ish* than we realize. There is something healthy and glorious buried in that impulse, of course—made in God's own image, we desire order and fairness rather than chaos. But that impulse, like every part of us, has been diseased by the ruinous fall into sin. Our capacity to apprehend the heart of God has gone into meltdown. We are left with an impoverished view of how he feels about his people, an impoverished view that (once more, due to sin) thinks it is in fact an expansive and accurate view of who he is—like a grandson who, shown a crisp one-hundred-dollar bill, concludes that his grandfather must be very wealthy, not knowing the billions in real estate of which that gift is just the tiniest reflection.

So God tells us in plain terms how tiny our natural views of his heart are. His thoughts are not our thoughts. His ways are not our ways. And not because we're just a few degrees off. No, "as high as the heavens are above the earth"—a Hebrew way of expressing spatial infinitude—"so are my ways higher than your ways and my thoughts than your thoughts" (v. 9). In verse 8 God says his ways and ours are different; in verse 9 he gets more specific and says his thoughts are higher. It's as if God is saying in verse 8 that he and we think very differently, whereas in verse 9 he is saying precisely how, namely, his "thoughts" (the Hebrew word doesn't merely mean "passing mental reflection" but "plans," "devices," "intentions," "purposes") are higher, grander, enveloped in a compassion for which we fallen sinners have no natural category.

There is only one other place in the Bible where we have the exact phrase "as high as the heavens are above the earth." In Psalm 103 David prays: "For as high as the heavens are above the earth, so great is his steadfast love toward those who fear him" (v. 11). The two passages—Psalm 103:11 and Isaiah 55:9—mutually illumine one another.[2] God's ways and thoughts are not our ways and thoughts in that his are thoughts of love and ways of compassion that stretch to a degree beyond our mental horizon.

2   The Hebrew text in both verses is *almost* identical, with just one difference in preposition, though the essential meaning remains the same.

———

Calvin—the theologian most famous for teaching on divine providence—saw that the mystery of providence is not what Isaiah 55 is really after. He notes that some interpret the phrase "my thoughts are not your thoughts" to be a sheer distancing between God and us, expressing the enormous gulf between sacred divinity and profane humanity. Yet Calvin saw that, in fact, the flow of the passage is in exactly the opposite direction. There is indeed a great distance between God and us; we think small thoughts of God's heart, but he knows his heart is inviolably, expansively, invincibly set on us.

"Because it is difficult to remove terror from trembling minds," Calvin comments, "Isaiah draws an argument from the nature of God, that he will be ready to pardon and to be reconciled."[3] Calvin then tunnels in to the core of what God is telling us in this text. After identifying the erroneous interpretation, he says:

> But the Prophet's meaning, I think, is different, and is more correctly explained, according to my judgment, by other commentators, who think that he draws a distinction between God's disposition and man's disposition. Men are wont to judge and measure God from themselves; for their hearts are moved by angry passions, and are very difficult to be appeased; and therefore they think that they cannot be reconciled to God, when they have once offended him. But the Lord shows that he is far from resembling men.[4]

3   Calvin, *Isaiah*, 168.
4   Calvin, *Isaiah*, 168. Calvin says something similar when commenting on Ps. 89:2: "Never will a man freely open his mouth to praise God, unless he is fully persuaded that God,

Calvin's language of God's disposition here is heart language. Remember, when we speak of God's heart, we're speaking of the spring-loaded tilt of his affections, his natural bent, the regular flow of who he is and what he does. And the divine disposition, teaches Calvin, is, according to Isaiah 55, the photo negative of our natural fallen disposition.

Our lethargic apprehensions of the uproarious joy of divine pardoning lower the ceiling on whom we perceive God to be, but they do not limit who God in fact is. "God is infinitely compassionate and infinitely ready to forgive, so that it ought to be ascribed exclusively to our unbelief, if we do not obtain pardon from him."[5]

———

God's heart of compassion confounds our intuitive predilections about how he loves to respond to his people if they would but dump in his lap the ruin and wreckage of their lives.

He isn't like you. Even the most intense of human love is but the faintest echo of heaven's cascading abundance. His heartful thoughts for you outstrip what you can conceive. He intends to restore you into the radiant resplendence for which you were created. And that is dependent not on you keeping yourself clean but on you taking your mess to him. He doesn't limit himself to working with the unspoiled parts of us that remain after a lifetime of sinning. His power runs so deep that he is able to redeem the very worst parts

even when he is angry with his people, never lays aside his fatherly affection towards them." John Calvin, *Commentary on the Book of Psalms*, vol. 3, trans. James Anderson (repr., Grand Rapids, MI: Baker, 2003), 420.

5 Calvin, *Isaiah*, 169. Goodwin likewise reflects on Isa. 55:8–9 in *The Works of Thomas Goodwin*, 12 vols. (repr., Grand Rapids, MI: Reformation Heritage, 2006), 2:194.

of our past into the most radiant parts of our future. But we need to take those dark miseries to him.

We know that he is the future restorer of the undeserving because of what the passage goes on to say:

> For you shall go out in joy
> and be led forth in peace;
> the mountains and the hills before you
> shall break forth into singing,
> and all the trees of the field shall clap their hands.
> Instead of the thorn shall come up the cypress;
> instead of the brier shall come up the myrtle;
> and it shall make a name for the LORD,
> an everlasting sign that shall not be cut off. (Isa. 55:12–13)

God's thoughts are so much higher than ours that not only does he abundantly pardon the penitent; he has determined to bring his people into a future so glorious we can hardly bring ourselves to dare hope for it. The poetry of this passage is beautifully communicating that God's heart for his people is building toward a crescendo as the generations roll by, preparing to explode onto human history at the end of all things. Our joyous restored humanity will surge forward with such spiritually nuclear energy that the creation itself will erupt in raucous hymns of celebration. This is the party for which the created order is on the edge of its seat in eager anticipation (Rom. 8:19), because its glory is bound up with and dependent on our glory (Rom. 8:21). The universe will be rinsed clean and restored to sparkling brightness and dignity as the sons and daughters of God step into a future as secure as it is undeserved.

How can we be so certain?

Because although his ways are higher than our ways, the *way* in which his thoughts are higher than ours is that we do not realize just how low he delights to come. As we read a few chapters later in Isaiah:

> Thus says the One who is high and lifted up,
>> who inhabits eternity, whose name is Holy:
> "I dwell in the high and holy place,
>> and also with him who is of a contrite and lowly spirit,
> to revive the spirit of the lowly,
>> and to revive the heart of the contrite." (57:15)

Where is the heart of God, the unspeakably exalted one, naturally drawn, according to Isaiah 57:15? To the lowly. When Jesus showed up seven hundred years after Isaiah prophesied and revealed his deepest heart as "gentle and lowly," he was proving once and for all that gentle lowliness is indeed where God loves to dwell. It is what he does. It is who he is. His ways are not our ways.

18

Yearning Bowels

My heart yearns for him.
JEREMIAH 31:20

THE HIGH POINT OF JEREMIAH'S prophecy is chapters 30–33. Scholars call this "the Book of Consolation" because God reveals to his people in these chapters his final response to their sinfulness, and it is not what they deserve. Expecting judgment, he surprises them with comfort. Why? Because he had pulled them into his heart, and they cannot sin their way out of it. "I have loved you with an everlasting love," he assures them (Jer. 31:3).

What does the Book of Consolation come on the heels of? Twenty-nine chapters of sordid recounting of Israel's sinfulness. To take a single representative statement from the opening chapters:

- "I will declare my judgments against them, for all their evil." (1:16)
- "My people have forsaken me." (2:13)
- "You have polluted the land with your vile whoredom." (3:2)

- "O Jerusalem, how long shall your wicked thoughts lodge within you?" (4:14)
- "This people has a stubborn and rebellious heart." (5:23)
- "As a well keeps its water fresh, so she keeps fresh her evil." (6:7)

And so on through twenty-nine chapters. And then, on the other side of chapters 30–33, the rest of the book is judgment against the nations.

But here at the center of the book, the pinnacle from which the whole fifty-two-chapter book can be viewed, is the Book of Consolation. And within these four chapters, perhaps the text that sums it all up best is 31:20:

> Is Ephraim my dear son?
>> Is he my darling child?
> For as often as I speak against him,
>> I do remember him still.
> Therefore my heart yearns for him;
>> I will surely have mercy on him,
>> declares the LORD.

"Ephraim" is just another term for Israel, God's people, though it appears to be a sort of divine term of affection for Israel throughout the Old Testament. And God asks, "Is he my darling child?" God is not wondering. It's a declaration, clothed in the gentleness of a question. His people are his "dear son" and even his "darling child." Does your doctrine of God have room for him speaking like that?

"For as often as I speak against him"—as he has for twenty-nine chapters, scathingly upbraiding his people—"I do remember him still." *Remember* here is not faculty of recall. This is God. He is all-knowing. He holds all truth about all things in all times in his mind with equal, perfect knowledge. *Remember* here is covenant language. It is relational. This is remembering not as the alternative to forgetting but as the alternative to *forsaking*.

And then comes the high point of the key verse of the four-chapter center of the book of Jeremiah: "Therefore my heart yearns for him."

———

"My heart." There is another Hebrew word for "heart," *lev* (pronounced lāve), which is the typical underlying Hebrew word for "heart" in the Old Testament (such as in Lam. 3:33: "he does not afflict from his *heart*"). But here in Jeremiah 31 the word is *meah*. It literally refers to the insides of a person, the guts. This is why older translations such as the KJV render it "bowels." It is the word used, for example, in 2 Samuel 20:10, when Joab stabs Amasa "in the stomach and spilled his *entrails* to the ground."

God, of course, does not have guts. It is his way of speaking of his innermost reflex, his churning insides, his deepest feelings of which our emotions are an image—in a word, as the text renders it, his heart. Calvin reminds us that to speak of God's bowels or heart "does not properly belong to God," but this in no way dilutes the truth that God is communicating truly "the greatness of his love towards us."[1]

Note what the text says his heart does. "My heart *yearns* for him." What is it to yearn? It is something different than to bless or to save or even to love. The Hebrew word here (*hamah*) at its root has a denotation of being restless or agitated, or even growling or

———

1 John Calvin, *Commentaries on the Prophet Jeremiah and the Lamentations*, vol. 4, trans. J. Owen (repr., Grand Rapids, MI: Baker, 2003), 109.

roaring or being boisterous or turbulent. Do you see what God is revealing about himself, what he is insisting on? His capacious affections for his own are not threatened by their fickleness, because pouring out of his heart is the turbulence of divine longing. And what God wants, God gets.

Therefore: "I will surely have mercy on him." If you were to translate that literally, it would awkwardly be something like: "Having mercy I will have mercy on him." Sometimes Hebrew doubles up a verb to be emphatic (the same construction occurs earlier in the verse with "remember"). The yearning heart of God delivers and redelivers sinners who find themselves drowning in the sewage of their life, twenty-nine chapters deep, in need of a rescue that they cannot even begin on their own, let alone complete.

Whom do you perceive him to be, *in* your sin and your suffering? Who do you think God is—not just on paper but in the kind of person you believe is hearing you when you pray? How does he feel about you? His saving of us is not cool and calculating. It is a matter of yearning—not yearning for the Facebook you, the you that you project to everyone around you. Not the you that you wish you were. Yearning for the real you. The you underneath everything you present to others.

We need to understand that however long we have been walking with the Lord, whether we have never read the whole Bible or have a PhD in it, we have a perverse resistance to this. Out of his heart flows mercy; out of ours, reluctance to receive it. We are the cool and calculating ones, not he. He is open-armed. We stiff-arm. Our naturally decaffeinated views of God's heart might feel right because we're being stern with ourselves, not letting ourselves off the hook too easily. Such sternness feels appropriately morally serious. But this deflecting of God's yearning heart does not reflect Scripture's testimony about how God feels toward his own. God is of course morally serious, far more than we are. But the Bible takes us by the hand and leads us out from under the feeling that his heart for us wavers according to our loveliness. God's heart confounds our intuitions of who he is.

Thomas Goodwin quotes Jeremiah 31:20 and then deduces that if this is true of God, how much more of Christ. He explains that such a text "may afford us the strongest consolations and encouragements" in the presence of many sins in our lives:

> There is comfort concerning such infirmities, in that your very sins move him to pity more than to anger. . . . Christ takes part with you, and is far from being provoked against you, as all his anger is turned upon your sin to ruin it; yea, his pity is increased the more towards you, even as the heart of a father is to a child that has some loathsome disease, or as one is to a member of his body that has leprosy, he hates not the member, for it is his flesh, but the disease, and that provokes him to pity the part affected the more. What shall not make for us, when our sins, that are both against Christ and us, shall be turned as motives to him to pity us the more?[2]

Goodwin explains that our pity and compassion are drawn out in corresponding intensity to the degree to which we love the one in view. "The greater the misery is, the more is the pity when the party is beloved. Now of all miseries, sin is the greatest," and "Christ will look upon it as such." How then does he respond to such ugliness

---

2 Thomas Goodwin, *The Heart of Christ* (Edinburgh: Banner of Truth, 2011), 155–56.

in our lives? "And he, loving your persons, and hating only the sin, his hatred shall all fall, and that only upon the sin, to free you of it by its ruin and destruction, but his affections shall be the more drawn out to you; and this as much when you lie under sin as under any other affliction. Therefore fear not."[3]

———

Some of us separate out our sins from our sufferings. We are culpable for our sins, after all, whereas our suffering (much of it anyway) is simply what befalls us in this world ruined by the fall. So we tend to have greater difficulty expecting God's gentle compassion toward our sins in the same way as toward our sufferings. Surely his heart flows more freely when I am sinned against than when I myself sin?

But observe Goodwin's logic. If the intensity of love maps onto the intensity of misery in the one beloved, and if our greatest misery is our sinfulness, then God's most intense love flows down to us in our sinfulness. Yes, God has hatred, Goodwin says—toward sin. And the combination of love for us plus hatred for sin equals the most omnipotent certainty possible that he will see us through to final liberation from sin and unfiltered basking in his own joyous heart for us one day.

The world is starving for a yearning love, a love that remembers instead of forsakes. A love that isn't tied to our loveliness. A love that gets down underneath our messiness. A love that is bigger than the enveloping darkness we might be walking through even today. A love of which even the very best human romance is the faintest of whispers.

3   Goodwin, *Heart of Christ*, 156.

And yet this may seem so abstract, as Jeremiah speaks of God's heart—subjective, mushy, ethereal. But remember why Goodwin can move so seamlessly from the heart of God in Jeremiah to the heart of Christ. What if the abstract became concrete? What if the heart of God wasn't just something coming down on us from heaven, but something that showed up among us here on earth? What if we saw God's heart not in a prophet telling us words, but in a prophet telling us he *was* God's Word—the embodiment of all that God wanted to say to us?

If Jeremiah 31:20—"my heart yearns for him"—if those words were to get dressed in flesh, what might those words look like?

We need not wonder. It looks like a Middle Eastern carpenter restoring men's and women's dignity and humanity and health and conscience through healings and exorcisms and teaching and hugging and forgiving.

And now we begin to see resolution to the tension that Jeremiah 31:20 has built in to it, a tension that rumbles down through the entire Old Testament, building in momentum, growing in sharpness—the tension between divine justice and divine mercy. God says here, "I speak against him," but he also says, "I do remember him still." Indictment *and* love, justice *and* mercy—swiveling back and forth here, as we see all through the Old Testament.

But at the height of human history, justice was fully satisfied and mercy was fully poured out at the same time, when the Father sent his eternally "dear Son" and "darling child" to a Roman cross, where God truly did "speak against him," where Jesus Christ poured out his blood, the innocent for the guilty, so that God could say of us, "I remember him still." Even as he forsook Jesus himself.

On the cross, we see what God did to satisfy his yearning for us. He went that far. He went all the way. The blushing effusiveness of heaven's bowels funneled down into the crucifixion of Christ.

Repent of your small thoughts of God's heart. Repent and let him love you.

19

Rich in Mercy

But God, being rich in mercy . . .
EPHESIANS 2:4

THE WORKS OF THOMAS GOODWIN come down to us in twelve volumes, over five hundred pages each, in small font, densely written. And volume 2 is given entirely to Ephesians chapter 2. This volume is a series of sermons, and Goodwin slows way down when he comes to verse 4, giving several sermons to this single verse:

> But God, being rich in mercy, because of the great love with which he loved us . . .

Verses 1 through 3 tell us why we needed saving: we were spiritually dead. Verses 5 and 6 tell us what the saving was: God made us alive. But it's verse 4, right in the middle, that tells us why God saved us. Verses 1–3 are the problem; verses 5–6 are the solution; and verse 4 is the reason God actually went about fixing the problem rather than leaving us where we were.

And what is that reason? God is not poor in mercy. He is rich in mercy.

Nowhere else in the Bible is God described as rich in anything. The only thing he is called *rich* in is: mercy. What does this mean? It means that God is something other than what we naturally believe him to be. It means the Christian life is a lifelong shedding of tepid thoughts of the goodness of God. In his justice, God is exacting; in his mercy, God is overflowing. "He is rich unto all; that is, he is infinite, overflowing in goodness, he is good to a profuseness, he is good to the pouring forth of riches, he is good to an abundance."[1] Just as the Old Testament doubles up the verb "to have mercy" in Jeremiah 31:20, the New Testament calls God "rich in mercy."

Having probed in recent chapters Old Testament precursors to what explodes onto the scene of human history in Matthew 11:29, and at every turn in the four Gospels, we now return to the New Testament for our final few chapters.

Ephesians 2:4 says, "God, *being* rich in mercy . . ." *Being*, not *becoming*. A statement like that is taking us into the inner recesses of the Creator, into heaven's Holy of Holies, behind the inner veil, disclosing to us the animating center of God's very being and nature. "He is the spring of all mercy . . . it is natural to him. . . . It is his nature and disposition, because when he shows mercy, he does it with his whole heart."[2] This is why he *delights* in mercy (Mic. 7:18).

1   Thomas Goodwin, *The Works of Thomas Goodwin*, 12 vols. (repr., Grand Rapids, MI: Reformation Heritage, 2006), 2:182.
2   Goodwin, *Works*, 2:179.

This is why David acknowledged in prayer to God that the mercy shown him was "according to your own heart" (1 Chron. 17:19). He is a fountain of mercy. He is a billionaire in the currency of mercy, and the withdrawals we make as we sin our way through life cause his fortune to grow greater, not less.

How can that be? Because mercy is who he is. If mercy was something he simply had, while his deepest nature was something different, there would be a limit on how much mercy he could dole out. But if he is essentially merciful, then for him to pour out mercy is for him to act in accord with who he is. It is simply for him to be God. When God shows mercy, he is acting in a way that is true to himself. Once again, this does not mean he is *only* merciful. He is also perfectly just and holy. He is rightly wrathful against sin and sinners. Following Scripture's lead in how it talks about God, however, these attributes of moral standards do not reflect his deepest heart.

The text goes on to join God's rich-in-mercy nature with his great love: "God, being rich in mercy, because of the great love with which he loved us . . ." Consider what Goodwin says:

> Where there is but a mention made by way of supposition, or by way of query, whether God will part with or cast off any of his people or no; you shall find that he throws it away with the highest indignation, his love is so great. . . . He speaks with the highest detestation that there should be any such thought in God. . . . He is so possessed with love to his people that he will hear nothing to the contrary. . . . Yea, his love is so strong that if there be any accusation—if at any time sin or devil come to accuse,

it moves God to bless. His love is so violent, it is so set, that he takes occasion to bless so much the more.[3]

When the Scripture speaks of "the great love with which he loved us," we must see what Goodwin is helping us understand. Divine love is not forbearance or longsuffering or patience. Though God does forbear with us, his love is something deeper, something more active. His love is great because it surges forward all the more when the beloved is threatened, even if threatened as a result of its own folly. We understand this on a human level; an earthly father's love rises up within when he sees his child accused or afflicted, even if justly accused or deservingly afflicted. Renewed affection boils up within.

And that is where mercy comes in. He loves us—as Goodwin says repeatedly in one of his sermons on Ephesians 2:4—with an "invincible" love.[4] And as love rises, mercy descends. Great love fills his heart; rich mercy flows out of his heart.

Perhaps this all seems a little abstract. Mercy and love are rather vacuous concepts, after all. They sound nice but what do they actually mean in my own Monday blues, my Wednesday discouragements, my Friday night loneliness, my Sunday morning boredom?

Two thoughts may help, one regarding the need for this rich mercy, the other regarding the embodiment of this rich mercy.

————

First, the need for rich mercy. Ephesians 2:4 does not dangle out on its own. It is one bend in a mighty river flowing across the six

3   Goodwin, *Works*, 2:176.
4   Goodwin, *Works*, 2:170–80.

chapters of Ephesians. And the harrowing stretch just upstream of 2:4 goes like this:

> And you were dead in the trespasses and sins in which you once walked, following the course of this world, following the prince of the power of the air, the spirit that is now at work in the sons of disobedience—among whom we all once lived in the passions of our flesh, carrying out the desires of the body and the mind, and were by nature children of wrath, like the rest of mankind. (2:1–3)

Christ was sent not to mend wounded people or wake sleepy people or advise confused people or inspire bored people or spur on lazy people or educate ignorant people, but to raise dead people.

Consider the overall impact of these three verses. Paul is not speaking of sin the way we often do: "I messed up," "I made a mistake," "I'm struggling with . . ."; Paul identifies sin as the comprehensive, enveloping, inexorable flow of our lives. Our sins are less like an otherwise healthy man occasionally tripping up and more like a man who is disease-ridden from head to foot—or, if we take the language of Ephesians 2 seriously, dead.

We were following Satan ("the prince of the power of the air"), even if we didn't know it. The power of hell was not only something we yielded to, it was something inside us—"the spirit that is now at work *in* the sons of disobedience." We were "by nature children of wrath." Divine wrath was something so deserving, so attendant, that we were its very children. We didn't just occasionally slip into the passions of our flesh; we "lived in" those passions. It was the air we breathed. What water is to fish, inordinate ugliness of desire was to us. We inhaled rejection of God, and we exhaled self-destruction and well-deserved judgment. Beneath our smiles at the grocery store and cheerful greetings to the mailman we were quietly enthroning Self and eviscerating our souls of the beauty and dignity and worship for which they were made. Sin was not something we lapsed into; it defined our moment-by-moment existence at the level of deed, word, thought, and, yes, even desire—"carrying out the desires of the body and the mind." We not only lived in sin; we enjoyed living in sin. We wanted to live in sin. It was our coddled treasure, our Gollum's ring, our settled delight. In short, we were dead. Utterly helpless. That's what his mercy healed.

Well, you say, that really doesn't describe me. I grew up in a law-abiding home. We went to church. I kept my nose clean. I've never been arrested. I've been decent to my neighbors. But look at what Paul says: ". . . among whom *we all* once lived in the passions of our flesh."

Surely not. This is Paul the former Pharisee, the law keeper to end all law keepers, "a Hebrew of Hebrews; as to the law, a Pharisee; as to zeal, a persecutor of the church; as to righteousness under the law, blameless" (Phil. 3:5–6). How could he include himself among those who were devoted to the passions of the flesh? Neither of these is a one-time self-description, moreover. Multiple times in Acts, as in Philippians 3, Paul describes his earlier life as "according to the strict manner of our fathers" (Acts 22:3), or "according to the strictest party of our religion" (Acts 26:5), even from a young age (Acts 26:4). And yet, as in Ephesians 2, in Titus 3 he again identifies his former life as "foolish, disobedient, led astray, [enslaved] to various passions and pleasures" (Titus 3:3). So which was it?

The only way to make sense of these two kinds of passages is to understand that we can vent our fleshly passions by breaking all the rules, or we can vent our fleshly passions by keeping all the rules, but both ways of venting the flesh still need resurrection. We can be immoral dead people, or we can be moral dead people. Either way, we're dead.

The mercy of God reaches down and rinses clean not only obviously bad people but fraudulently good people, both of whom equally stand in need of resurrection.

God is rich in mercy. He doesn't withhold mercy from some kinds of sinners while extending it to others. Because mercy is who he is— "*being* rich in mercy"—his heart gushes forth mercy to sinners one and all. His mercy overcomes even the deadness of our souls and the hollowed-out, zombie-like existence that we are all naturally born into.

The mercy of Ephesians 2:4 does not seem far off and abstract when we feel the weight of our sin.

———

Second, the embodiment of rich mercy.

The richness of divine mercy becomes real to us not only when we see how depraved we naturally are, but also when we see that the river of mercy flowing out of God's heart took shape as a man. Perhaps the notion of heavenly mercy seems abstract; but what if that mercy became something we could see, hear, and touch?

That is what happened in the incarnation. When Paul speaks of the saving appearance of Christ, he says, "When grace appeared . . ." (Titus 2:11). The grace and mercy of God is so bound up with and manifested in Jesus himself that to speak of Christ appearing is to speak of grace appearing. "Christ is nothing but pure grace clothed with our nature," wrote Sibbes.[5]

---

5   Richard Sibbes, *The Church's Riches by Christ's Poverty*, in *The Works of Richard Sibbes*, ed. A. B. Grosart, 7 vols. (Edinburgh: Banner of Truth, 1983), 4:518.

Therefore when we look at the ministry of Christ in the four Gospels, we are seeing what "rich in mercy" looks like—how "rich in mercy" talks, how it conducts itself toward sinners, how it moves toward sufferers. Jesus not only proved that God is rich in mercy by going to the cross and dying in our place to secure that mercy. Jesus also shows us how God's richness in mercy actually looks and speaks.

To put it differently, God's love is "invincible" (to use Goodwin's word) because of Christ's coming. Later in Ephesians 2, at verse 6, Paul says we are, right now, seated with Christ in heaven. That means that if you are in Christ, you are as eternally invincible as he is. Sibbes said, "Whatsoever Christ is freed from, I am freed from it. It can no more hurt me than it can hurt him now in heaven."[6] For God to de-resurrect you, to bring his rich mercy to an end, Jesus Christ himself would have to be sucked down out of heaven and put back in the tomb of Joseph of Arimathea. You're that safe.

———

Consider God's richness in mercy for your own life.

He doesn't meet you halfway. His very nature is to engage death and bring life. He did that decisively once and for all at your conversion, but he continues to do it time and again in your sin and folly. "After our calling, how do we provoke God!" preached Goodwin. "It is so with all Christians. . . . Yet saved [we are], because the love of God is invincible, it overcomes all difficulties."[7]

Perhaps, looking at the evidence of your life, you do not know what to conclude except that this mercy of God in Christ has passed

6 Sibbes, *Works*, 4:504.
7 Goodwin, *Works*, 2:175.

you up. Maybe you have been deeply mistreated. Misunderstood. Betrayed by the one person you should have been able to trust. Abandoned. Taken advantage of. Perhaps you carry a pain that will never heal till you are dead. *If my life is any evidence of the mercy of God in Christ*, you might think, *I'm not impressed.*

To you I say, the evidence of Christ's mercy toward you is not your life. The evidence of his mercy toward you is his—mistreated, misunderstood, betrayed, abandoned. Eternally. In your place.

If God sent his own Son to walk through the valley of condemnation, rejection, and hell, you can trust him as you walk through your own valleys on your way to heaven.

Perhaps you have difficulty receiving the rich mercy of God in Christ not because of what others have done to you but because of what you've done to torpedo your life, maybe through one big, stupid decision or maybe through ten thousand little ones. You have squandered his mercy, and you know it.

To you I say, do you know what Jesus does with those who squander his mercy? He pours out more mercy. God is rich in mercy. That's the whole point.

Whether we have been sinned against or have sinned ourselves into misery, the Bible says God is not tightfisted with mercy but openhanded, not frugal but lavish, not poor but rich.

That God is rich in mercy means that your regions of deepest shame and regret are not hotels through which divine mercy passes but homes in which divine mercy abides.

It means the things about you that make you cringe most, make him hug hardest.

It means his mercy is not calculating and cautious, like ours. It is unrestrained, flood-like, sweeping, magnanimous.

It means our haunting shame is not a problem for him, but the very thing he loves most to work with.

It means our sins do not cause his love to take a hit. Our sins cause his love to surge forward all the more.

It means on that day when we stand before him, quietly, unhurriedly, we will weep with relief, shocked at how impoverished a view of his mercy-rich heart we had.

20

Our Law-ish Hearts,
His Lavish Heart

The Son of God, who loved me . . .
GALATIANS 2:20

THERE ARE TWO WAYS to live the Christian life. You can live it either *for* the heart of Christ or *from* the heart of Christ. You can live for the smile of God or from it. For a new identity as a son or daughter of God or from it. For your union with Christ or from it.

The battle of the Christian life is to bring your own heart into alignment with Christ's, that is, getting up each morning and replacing your natural orphan mind-set with a mind-set of full and free adoption into the family of God through the work of Christ your older brother, who loved you and gave himself for you out of the overflowing fullness of his gracious heart.

Picture a twelve-year-old boy growing up in a healthy, loving family. As he matures, through no fault of his parents he finds himself trying to figure out how to really assure himself a place in the family.

One week he tries to create a new birth certificate for himself. The next week he determines to spend all his extra time scrubbing the kitchen clean. The following week he determines to do all he can to imitate his dad. One day his parents question his strange behavior. "I'm just doing all I can to secure my place in the family, guys!" How would his father respond? "Calm yourself, my dear son! There's nothing you could possibly do to earn your place among us. You are our son. Period. You didn't do anything at the start to get into our family, and you can't do anything now to get out of our family. Live your life knowing your sonship is settled and irreversible."

The purpose of this chapter, through reflecting on the book of Galatians, is to bring the heart of Christ to bear on our chronic tendency to function out of a subtle belief that our obedience strengthens the love of God. We act like that twelve-year-old. And our Father responds with corrective love.

———

Galatians teaches that we are made right with God based on what Christ has done rather than on what we do. To help the gospel, therefore, is to lose the gospel. But the central burden of the letter is not about learning that for the first time in conversion but about how easily we slip away from that as believers. Paul's perplexed question is, "Having begun by the Spirit, are you now being perfected by the flesh?" (Gal. 3:3). The central message of Galatians is that the freeness of God's grace and love is not only the gateway but also the pathway of the Christian life.[1]

---

1   Luther is especially clear on this in his justly famous commentary on Galatians. Martin Luther, *Galatians*, Crossway Classic Commentaries, ed. A. McGrath and J. I. Packer (Wheaton, IL: Crossway, 1998).

In the course of the letter Paul explains the doctrine of justification by faith in order to help the Galatians live healthy Christian
lives. Justification represents the objective side of our salvation.
But Paul also speaks of the subjective side of salvation, the love of
Christ, such as when he speaks of "the Son of God, who loved me
and gave himself for me" (2:20). A healthy Christian life is built
on both the objective and the subjective sides of the gospel—the
justification that flows from the work of Christ, and the love that
flows from the heart of Christ.

But the two are related. In March 1767 the pastor and hymn
writer John Newton wrote a letter to a friend and said:

> Are not you amazed sometimes that you should have so much
> as a hope, that, poor and needy as you are, the Lord thinks of
> you? But let not all you feel discourage you. For if our Physician
> is almighty, our disease cannot be desperate and if He casts none
> out that come to Him, why should you fear? Our sins are many,
> but His mercies are more: our sins are great, but His righteousness
> is greater: we are weak, but He is power. Most of our complaints
> are owing to unbelief, and the remainder of a legal spirit.[2]

Note the way Newton speaks of the way "that, poor and needy
as you are, the Lord thinks of you," and the fact that (alluding to
John 6:37, explored earlier, in chapter 6) "He casts none out that
come to Him." Newton is getting at Christ's heart here. And look
at what he diagnoses as the bottom-line source of our resistance to
these assurances: "a legal spirit." That's an eighteenth-century way

2 John Newton, *Cardiphonia*, in *The Works of John Newton*, 2 vols. (New York: Robert
   Carter, 1847), 1:343.

of referring to works righteousness or legalism, the inveterate yet subtle proclivity to seek to leverage Christ's favor with our behavior.

Newton helps us see that one reason we have a diminished awareness of the heart of Christ is that we are blindly operating out of a legal spirit. We don't see just how natural it is to us to operate out of works righteousness. But this kills our sense of Christ's heart for us because this legal spirit filters our sense of his heart according to how we are spiritually performing. Think of a vent in your bedroom that's connected to your furnace. If you keep that vent closed on a cold winter day, the heat will be circulating throughout the ducts in your home, but you will not experience warmth because you're closing it off. Opening the vent floods your room with warmth. The heat was already there, waiting to be accessed. But you were not benefiting from it.

Galatians exists to open the vents of our hearts to the felt grace of God.

———

But isn't that love and grace pretty basic? Don't we Christians know that already?

Yes and no. In Galatians 3:10 Paul says something striking that is easy to miss. Our English text tells us that "all who rely on works of the law are under a curse." The passage goes on to explain that this is because, if we are going to try to get justified according to our performance, we'll have to perform perfectly. Once we sign up for the law approach to salvation, the slightest failure torpedoes the whole project.

Let's consider what Paul means when he says that "all who rely on works of the law are under a curse" (3:10). The text literally reads:

"As many as are *of* works of law are under a curse." To "rely on" our works is a good rendering, but consider what it is to be *of* works (Paul uses the same phrase in Romans 9:32 when speaking of Israel pursuing the law "as of works"). Paul doesn't say that those who *do* works are under a curse. He says those who are of works are under a curse. Doubtless there is overlap here, and doing is included to some degree. But he speaks of being *of works*.

Paul is exposing who we most deeply are. Not, what do you assent to doctrinally? But, what are you of? To be of works is not to fall short. It is to march in the wrong direction. It is a certain spirit, a legal spirit.

As the gospel sinks in more deeply over time, and we wade ever deeper into the heart of Christ, one of the first outer shells of our old life that the gospel pierces is the *doing* of works unto approval. But there is another, deeper level, an instinct or "of-ness" level, that must be deconstructed and shed too. We can go through the whole day trumpeting the futility of doing works to please God, all the while saying the right thing from an "of works" heart. And our natural "of-works-ness" reflects not only a resistance to the doctrine of justification by faith but also, even more deeply, a resistance to Christ's very heart.

———

There is an entire psychological substructure that, due to the fall, is a near-constant manufacturing of relational leveraging, fear-stuffing, nervousness, score-keeping, neurotic controlling, anxiety-festering silliness that is not something we say or even think so much as something we exhale. You can smell it on people, though some of us are good at hiding it. And if you trace this fountain of scurrying haste, in all its various manifestations, down to the root, you don't find childhood difficulties or a Myers-Briggs diagnosis or Freudian impulses. You find gospel deficit. You find lack of felt awareness of Christ's heart. All the worry and dysfunction and resentment are the natural fruit of living in a mental universe of law. The felt love of Christ really is what brings rest, wholeness, flourishing, shalom— that existential calm that for brief, gospel-sane moments settles over you and lets you step in out of the storm of of-works-ness. You see for a moment that in Christ you truly are invincible. The verdict really is in; nothing can touch you. He has made you his own and will never cast you out.

Living out of a law-fueled subconscious resistance to Christ's heart, which we all tend to think we're successfully avoiding (those silly Galatians!), is deep and subtle and pervasive. It is more pervasive than the occasional moments of self-conscious works-righteousness would indicate. Those moments of self-knowledge are indeed gifts of grace and not to be ignored. But they are only the visible tip of an invisible iceberg. They are surface symptoms. Law-ish-ness, of-works-ness, is by its very nature undetectable because it's natural, not unnatural, to us. It feels normal. "Of works" to fallen people is what water is to a fish.

And what does the gospel say? It puts the following words in each of our mouths: "the Son of God . . . loved me and gave himself for me." His heart for *me* could not sit still in heaven. Our sins darken our feelings of his gracious heart, but his heart cannot be diminished for his own people due to their sins any more than the sun's existence can be threatened due to the passing of a few wispy clouds or even an extended thunderstorm. The sun is shining. It cannot stop. Clouds, no clouds—sin, no sin—the tender heart of the Son of God is shining on me. This is an unflappable affection.

And the sweep of New Testament teaching is that it is the sun of Christ's heart, not the clouds of my sins, that now defines me. When we are united to Christ, Christ's punishment at the cross becomes my punishment. In other words, the end-time judgment that awaits all humans has, for those in Christ, already taken place. We who are in Christ no longer look to the future for judgment, but to the past; at the cross, we see our punishment happening, all our sins being punished in Jesus. The loved and restored you therefore trumps, outstrips, swallows up, the unrestored you. Not the other way around.

And the Christian life is simply the process of bringing my sense of self, my Identity with a capital "I," the ego, my swirling internal world of fretful panicky-ness arising out of that gospel deficit, into alignment with the more fundamental truth. The gospel is the invitation to let the heart of Christ calm us into joy, for we've already been discovered, included, brought in. We can bring our up-and-down moral performance into subjection to the settled fixedness of what Jesus feels about us.

We are sinners. We sin—not just in the past but in the present, and not only by our disobedience but by our "of-works" obedience. We are perversely resistant to letting Christ love us. But as Flavel says, "Why should you be such an enemy to your own peace? Why read over the evidences of God's love to your soul . . . ? Why do you study evasions, and turn off those comforts which are due to you?"[3]

---

3   John Flavel, *Keeping the Heart: How to Maintain Your Love for God* (Fearn, Scotland: Christian Focus, 2012), 94.

In the gospel, we are free to receive the comforts that are due us. Don't turn them off. Open the vent of your heart to the love of Christ, who loved you and gave himself for you.

Our law-ish hearts relax as his lavish heart comes home to us.

21

He Loved Us Then;
He'll Love Us Now

God shows his love for us . . .
ROMANS 5:8

IT IS ONE THING TO BELIEVE that God has put away and forgiven all our old failures that occurred before new birth. That is a
wonder of mercy, unspeakably rich; but those were, after all, sins
committed while we were still in the dark. We had not been made
new creatures, freshly empowered to walk in the light and honor
the Lord with our lives.

It's another thing to believe that God continues, just as freely, to
put away all our present failures that occur after new birth.

Perhaps, as believers today, we know God loves us. We really
believe that. But if we were to more closely examine how we actually relate to the Father moment by moment—which reveals our
actual theology, whatever we say we believe on paper—many of us
tend to believe it is a love infected with disappointment. He loves

us; but it's a flustered love. We see him looking down on us with paternal affection but slightly raised eyebrows: "How are they still falling short so much after all I have done for them?" we picture him wondering. We are now sinning "against light," the Puritans would say; we know the truth, and our hearts have been fundamentally transformed, and still we fall. And the shoulders of our soul remain drooped in the presence of God. Once again, it is a result of projecting our own capacities to love onto God. We do not know his truest heart.

And that is why Romans 5:6–11 is in the Bible:

> For while we were still weak, at the right time Christ died for the ungodly. For one will scarcely die for a righteous person—though perhaps for a good person one would dare even to die—but God shows his love for us in that while we were still sinners, Christ died for us. Since, therefore, we have now been justified by his blood, much more shall we be saved by him from the wrath of God. For if while we were enemies we were reconciled to God by the death of his Son, much more, now that we are reconciled, shall we be saved by his life. More than that, we also rejoice in God through our Lord Jesus Christ, through whom we have now received reconciliation.

———

A Christian conscience is a sensitized conscience. Now that we know God as Father, now that our eyes have been opened to our treasonous rebellion against our Creator, we feel more deeply than ever the ugliness of sin. Failure makes the soul cringe like never before. And so, following a paragraph rejoicing in the blessings of God's gracious redemption of sinners (Rom. 5:1–5), Paul pauses to convince us of how we can be assured of God's presence and favor going forward (5:6–11).

No less than three times in this second paragraph in Romans 5, Paul says roughly the same thing:

> *While we were still weak*, at the right time Christ died for the ungodly. (5:6)
> *While we were still sinners*, Christ died for us. (5:8)
> If *while we were enemies* we were reconciled to God by the death of his Son . . . (5:10)

To say the same truth backward: Jesus didn't die for us once we became strong (5:6); he didn't die for us once we started to overcome our sinfulness (5:8); God did not reconcile us to himself once we became friendly toward him (5:10).

God didn't meet us halfway. He refused to hold back, cautious, assessing our worth. That is not his heart. He and his Son took the initiative. On terms of grace and grace alone. In defiance of what we deserved. When we, despite our smiles and civility, were running from God as fast as we could, building our own kingdoms and loving our own glory, lapping up the fraudulent pleasures of the world, repulsed by the beauty of God and shutting up our ears at his calls to come home—it was then, in the hollowed-out horror of that revolting existence, that the prince of heaven bade his adoring angels farewell. It was then that he put himself into the murderous hands of these very rebels in a divine strategy planned from eternity past to rinse muddy sinners clean and hug them into his own heart despite their squirmy attempt to get free and scrub themselves clean on their own. Christ went down into death—"voluntary endurance of unutterable anguish,"[1] Warfield calls it—while we applauded. We couldn't have cared less. We were weak. Sinners. Enemies.

It was only after the fact, only once the Holy Spirit came flooding into our hearts, that the realization swept over us: he walked through *my* death. And he didn't simply die. He was condemned. He didn't simply leave heaven for me; he endured hell for me. He, not deserving to be condemned, absorbed it in my place—I, who alone deserved it. *That* is his heart. And into our empty souls, like a glass of cold water to a thirsty mouth, God poured his Holy Spirit to internalize the actual experience of God's love (v. 5).

What was the purpose of this heavenly rescue mission? "God shows his love for us . . ." (v. 8). The Greek word for "shows" here means to commend demonstrably, to hold forth, to bring into clear view, to put beyond questioning. In Christ's death, God is confronting our dark thoughts of him and our chronic insistence that divine love must have an endpoint, a limit, a point at which it finally runs dry. Christ died to confound our intuitive assumptions that divine love has an expiration date. He died to prove that God's love is, as Jonathan Edwards put it, "an ocean without shores or bottom."[2] God's love is as boundless as God himself. This is why the apostle Paul speaks of divine love as a reality that stretches to an immeasurable "breadth and length and height and depth" (Eph. 3:18)—the only thing in the universe as immeasurable as that is God himself. God's love is as expansive as God himself.

1   B. B. Warfield, *The Person and Work of Christ* (Oxford, UK: Benediction Classics, 2015), 134.

2   Jonathan Edwards, "That God Is the Father of Lights," in *The Blessing of God: Previously Unpublished Sermons of Jonathan Edwards*, ed. Michael McMullen (Nashville, TN: Broadman, 2003), 350.

For God to cease to love his own, God would need to cease to exist, because God does not simply have love; he is love (1 John 4:16). In the death of Christ for us sinners, God intends to put his love for us beyond question.

———

This is the greatest news in the history of the world. But even this is not Paul's main burden in verses 6 to 11. He's after something else.

What's the ultimate point Paul is driving at in Romans 5:6–11? Not God's past work, mainly. Paul's deepest burden is our present security, given that past work. He raises Christ's past work to drive home this point: if God did that back then, when you were so screwy and had zero interest in him, then what are you worried about now? The central burden of verses 6 through 11 is captured in the "since" of verse 9 (notice the way the whole paragraph swivels at this point): "*Since*, therefore, we have now been justified by his blood"—and now we hear Paul's driving concern—"much more shall we be saved by him from the wrath of God." Verse 10 drives the point even further home: "For if while we were enemies we were reconciled to God by the death of his Son"—and here's the point again—"much more, now that we are reconciled, shall we be saved by his life."

The language of being "saved" in verses 9 and 10 looks ahead to final salvation, referring not to the moment of conversion in this life but entrance into the presence of God in the next. Paul is saying that it is impossible to be truly justified at conversion without God looking after us right into heaven. Conversion isn't a fresh start. Conversion, authentic regeneration, is the invincibilizing of our future. We were enemies when God came to us and justified us; how much more will God care for us now that we are friends—indeed, sons? As John Flavel put it, "As God did not at first choose you because you were high, he will not now forsake you because you are low."[3]

How easily we who have been united to Christ wonder what God thinks of us in our failures now. The logic of Romans 5 is: Through his Son he drew near to us when we hated him. Will he remain distant now that we hope we can please him?

He eagerly suffered for us when we were failing, as orphans. Will he cross his arms over our failures now that we are his adopted children?

His heart was gentle and lowly toward us when we were lost. Will his heart be anything different toward us now that we are found?

While we were still . . . He loved us in our mess then. He'll love us in our mess now. Our very agony in sinning is the fruit of our adoption. A cold heart would not be bothered. We are not who we were.

When you sin, do a thorough job of repenting. Re-hate sin all over again. Consecrate yourself afresh to the Holy Spirit and his pure ways. But reject the devil's whisper that God's tender heart for you has grown a little colder, a little stiffer. He is not flustered by your sinfulness. His deepest disappointment is with your tepid thoughts of his heart. Christ died, placarding before you the love of God.

If you are in Christ—and only a soul in Christ would be troubled at offending him—your waywardness does not threaten your place in the love of God any more than history itself can be undone. The hardest part has been accomplished. God has already executed everything needed to secure your eternal happiness, and he did

---

3 John Flavel, *Keeping the Heart: How to Maintain Your Love for God* (Fearn, Scotland: Christian Focus, 2012), 43.

that while you were an orphan. Nothing can now un-child you. Not even you. Those in Christ are eternally imprisoned within the tender heart of God. We will be less sinful in the next life than we are now, but we will not be any more secure in the next life than we are now. If you are united to Christ, you are as good as in heaven already. As Spurgeon preached:

> Christ loved you before all worlds; long ere the day star flung his ray across the darkness, before the wing of angel had flapped the unnavigated ether, before aught of creation had struggled from the womb of nothingness, God, even our God, had set his heart upon all his children.
>
> Since that time, has he once swerved, has he once turned aside, once changed? No; ye who have tasted of his love and know his grace, will bear me witness, that he has been a certain friend in uncertain circumstances. . . .
>
> You have often left him; has he ever left you? You have had many trials and troubles; has he ever deserted you? Has he ever turned away his heart, and shut up his bowels of compassion? No, children of God, it is your solemn duty to say "No," and bear witness to his faithfulness.[4]

4   Charles Spurgeon, "A Faithful Friend," in *Sermons of C. H. Spurgeon* (New York: Sheldon, Blakeman, 1857), 13–14.

22

To the End

Having loved his own who were in the
world, he loved them to the end.

JOHN 13:1

"LOVE IN CHRIST DECAYS NOT," wrote Bunyan, "nor can be tempted so to do by anything that happens, or that shall happen hereafter, in the object so beloved."[1] What we are seeing in these past few chapters is that the heart of Christ for sinners and sufferers does not flash with tenderness occasionally or temporarily, sputtering out over time. Gentleness and lowliness of heart is who Christ is steadily, consistently, everlastingly, when all loveliness in us has withered.

How do we know?

We know because of what John 13:1 says, which the final few chapters of all four Gospel accounts narrate: Jesus came to the cliff of the cross and didn't change his mind. He walked over the edge.

---

1   John Bunyan, *The Saints' Knowledge of the Love of Christ*, in *The Works of John Bunyan*, ed. G. Offor, 3 vols. (repr., Edinburgh: Banner of Truth, 1991), 2:17.

Proportionally, John's Gospel devotes more space to the final week of Jesus's life than any other Gospel. And it is the first verse of chapter 13 that kicks off this final extended section to this Gospel. John's statement that Jesus loved his own to the end launches the passion narrative, and the arraignment and crucifixion of Christ is the historical demonstration of what is put in a nutshell in John 13:1. And John's point in 13:1 is that in going to the cross, Jesus did not retain something for himself, the way we tend to do when we seek to love others sacrificially. He does not love like us.

We love until we are betrayed. Jesus continued to the cross despite betrayal. We love until we are forsaken. Jesus loved through forsakenness.

We love up to a limit. Jesus loves to the end.

———

What is John 13:1 saying to sinners and sufferers with that little phrase "to the end"? It is a similar point to the first half of Romans 5, which we considered in the previous chapter. There the focus is more objective, as Paul develops his doctrine of justification from Romans 3 through the end of Romans 5. Here in John's Gospel we find a similar reassurance, but it is more subjective, focusing on Jesus's love. Romans 5 tells us that to forsake us would be a breach of God's justice. John 13 tells us that to forsake us would be a breach of Christ's own heart.

We read:

Now before the Feast of the Passover, when Jesus knew that his hour had come to depart out of this world to the Father, having loved his own who were in the world, he loved them to the end. (John 13:1)

Jesus knows that this is the beginning of the end for him. He is entering the final chapter and deepest valley of his earthly ministry. He "knew that his hour had come to depart out of this world to the Father." John then pauses in a moment of moving reflection and looks back over Jesus's ministry and forward to the final week. Looking back, John says, Jesus had "loved his own who were in the world." Looking forward, "he loved them to the end."

His ministry to this point has been utterly demanding—he has been tired and hungry, physically; misunderstood and mistreated by his friends and family, relationally; cornered and accused by the religious elite, publicly. But what is all this compared to what now lay before him? What is a cold drizzle compared to drowning? What is a shouted insult when you are on your way to the guillotine?

For consider exactly what was impending. Jesus had done his Father's will unwaveringly. But throughout it all, he knew he had the pleasure and favor of his Father. It had been pronounced over him (Matt. 3:17; 17:5). Now his worst nightmare was about to wash over him. Hell itself—not metaphorically, but in actuality, the horror of condemnation and darkness and death—was opening its jaws.

What *happened* at the cross, for those of us who claim to be its beneficiaries?

It is beyond calculating comprehension, of course. A three-year-old cannot comprehend the pain a spouse feels when cheated on. How much less could we comprehend what it meant for God to funnel the cumulative judgment for all the sinfulness of his people down onto one man. But reflecting on what we feel toward, say, the perpetrator of some unthinkable act of abuse toward an innocent victim gives us a taste of what God felt toward Christ as he, the last Adam, stood in for the sins of God's people. The righteous human wrath we feel—the wrath we would be wrong *not* to feel—is a drop in the ocean of righteous divine wrath the Father unleashed.

After all, God punished Jesus not for the sin of just one person but many. What must it mean when Isaiah says of the servant that "the LORD has laid on him the iniquity *of us all*" (Isa. 53:6)? What was it for Christ to swallow down the cumulative twistedness, self-enthronement, natural God hatred, of the elect? What must it have been for the sum total of righteous divine wrath generated not just by one man's sin but "the iniquity of us all" to come crashing down on a single soul?

It's speculation, but for myself I cannot believe it was physical extremity that killed Christ. What is physical torture compared to the full weight of centuries of cumulative wrath absorption? That mountain of piled-up horrors? How did Jesus even retain sanity psychologically in absorbing the sum-total penalty of every lustful thought and deed coming from the hearts of God's people—and that is one sin among many? Perhaps it was sheer despair that broke him down into death. If he was sweating blood at the *thought* of God's abandonment (Luke 22:44), what was it like to go through with it? Would it not have been the withdrawal of God's love from his heart, not the withdrawal of oxygen from his lungs, that killed him? Who could hold up mental stability when drinking down what God's people deserved? "In the presence of this mental anguish," wrote Warfield, "the physical tortures of the crucifixion retire into the background, and we may well believe that our Lord, though he died on the cross, yet died not of the cross, but, as we commonly say, of a broken heart."[2] It was the suffering of Christ's heart that overwhelmed what his physical frame could handle.

New Testament scholar Richard Bauckham notes that while Psalm 22:1 ("My God, my God, why have you forsaken me?") was originally written in Hebrew, Jesus spoke it in Aramaic and thus was personally appropriating it.[3] Jesus wasn't simply repeating David's experience of a thousand years earlier as a convenient parallel expression. Rather, every anguished Psalm 22:1 cry across the millennia was being recapitulated and fulfilled and deepened in Jesus. His was the true Psalm 22:1 of which ours are the shadows. As the people of God, all our *feelings* of forsakenness funneled through an actual human heart in a single moment of anguished horror on Calvary, an actual forsakenness.

Who could possibly bear up beneath it? Who would not cry out and shut down?

When communion with God had been one's oxygen, one's meat and drink, throughout one's whole life, without a single moment of interruption by sin—to suddenly bear the unspeakable weight of all our sins? Who could survive that? To lose that depth of communion *was* to die. The great love at the heart of the universe was being rent in two. The world's Light was going out.[4]

---

2 B. B. Warfield, *The Person and Work of Christ* (Oxford, UK: Benediction Classics, 2015), 133.

3 Richard Bauckham, *Jesus and the God of Israel: God Crucified and Other Studies on the New Testament's Christology of Divine Identity* (Grand Rapids, MI: Eerdmans, 2008), 255–56.

4 This is not to say the Son lost his Father's love absolutely; the Trinity cannot be broken in that sense. And though three persons, this is still one God, so we must be careful how we speak about the relations between the Father and the Son. Instead it is to say that the experience of the Son *as a real human*, and standing in for all the elect, was

And in venting that righteous wrath God was not striking a morally neutral tree. He was splintering the Lovely One. Beauty and Goodness himself was being uglified and vilified. "Stricken, smitten by God . . ." (Isa. 53:4).

So that we ugly ones could be freely beautified, pardoned, calmed. Our heaven through his hell. Our entrance into Love through his loss of it.

This was what loving to the end meant. Passing through the horror of the cross and drinking down the flood of filth, the centuries of sin, all that is revolting even in our eyes.

———

But why would he go through with it? Why would he step down into the horror of hellish condemnation when he was the one person who didn't deserve it?

The text tells us. "Having *loved* his own . . . he *loved* them to the end." Bunyan takes us into the workings of this love:

> It is common for equals to love, and for superiors to be beloved; but for the King of princes, for the Son of God, for Jesus Christ to love man thus: this is amazing, and that so much the more, for that man the object of his love, is so low, so mean, so vile, so

to lose a sense of the love of God and an experienced open channel of communion with the Father. On this see especially Francis Turretin's *Institutes of Elenctic Theology*, 3 vols., trans. G. M. Giger, ed. J. T. Dennison (Phillipsburg, NJ: P&R, 1997), the fourteenth topic of which (in vol. 2) is "The Mediatorial Office of Christ," in which Turretin explains the cross as the loss of the experience of the Father's love but not the absolute loss of the Father's love. Following closely the language of the Passion narratives, the forsakenness on the cross should primarily be understood as a forsakenness of Jesus (representing sinful humanity) by God, not primarily the divine Son by the Father.

undeserving, and so inconsiderable, as by the scriptures, everywhere he is described to be.

He is called God, the King of glory. But the persons of him beloved, are called transgressors, sinners, enemies, dust and ashes, fleas, worms, shadows, vapors, vile, filthy, sinful, unclean, ungodly fools, madmen. And now is it not to be wondered at, and are we not to be affected herewith, saying, And will you set your eye upon such a one? But how much more when He will set his *heart* upon us?

Love in him is essential to his being. God is love; Christ is God; therefore Christ is love, *love naturally*. He may as well cease to be, as cease to love. . . .

Love from Christ requires no taking beauteousness in the object to be beloved. It can act of and from itself, without all such kind of dependencies. The Lord Jesus sets his heart to love them.[5]

Notice the way Bunyan speaks of Christ's love as a matter of his setting his heart upon us. When the apostle John tells us that Jesus loved his own to the end, John is pulling back the veil to allow us to peer into the depths of who Jesus is. His heart for his own is not like an arrow, shot quickly but soon falling to the ground; or a runner, quick out of the gate, soon slowing and faltering. His heart is an avalanche, gathering momentum with time; a wildfire, growing in intensity as it spreads.

This is not who Christ is indiscriminately. The text says it is "his own" whom he loves to the end. "His own" is a phrase used throughout John to refer to Christ's true disciples, the children of God. In John 10, for example, Jesus speaks of his followers as his

---

5 Bunyan, *Works*, 2:16–17; emphasis original.

GENTLE AND LOWLY

sheep and says he "calls his *own* sheep by name" (v. 3). To those who are not his own, Jesus is a fearful judge, one whose wrath cannot be assuaged or dampened; the Bible teaches that Jesus will one day be "revealed from heaven with his mighty angels in flaming fire, inflicting vengeance on those who do not know God and on those who do not obey the gospel of our Lord Jesus" (2 Thess. 1:7–8). That passage goes on to say those who do not belong to Christ "will suffer the punishment of eternal destruction" (1:9).

But for his own, Jesus himself endured that punishment. He set his heart on his own. They are his. "There is not the meanest, the weakest, the poorest believer on the earth," wrote Owen, "but Christ prizes him more than all the world."[6]

Christ loved his own all the way through death itself. What must that mean for you? It means, first, that your future is secure. If you are his, heaven and relief is coming, for you cannot be made un-his. He himself made you his own, and you can't squirm out of his grasp.

And it means, second, that he will love *you* to the end. Not only is your future secure, on the basis of his death; your present is secure, proven in his heart. He will love you to the end because he cannot bear to do otherwise. No exit strategy. No prenup. He'll love to the end—"to the end of their lives, to the end of their sins, to the end of their temptations, to the end of their fears."[7]

6 John Owen, *Communion with God* (Fearn, Scotland: Christian Heritage, 2012), 218.
7 John Bunyan, *The Work of Jesus Christ as an Advocate*, in *Works*, 1:201.

23

Buried in His Heart Forevermore

*. . . so that in the coming ages he might show the
immeasurable riches of his grace in kindness toward us.*

EPHESIANS 2:7

WHAT'S THE MEANING OF EVERYTHING? What's the *telos*, the aim,
the macro reason and goal, for our small, ordinary lives?

We are on solid footing, both biblically and historically, if we
answer: "To glorify God."

After all, what else is there? We are pieces of art, designed to
be beautiful and thus draw attention to our artist. We are simply
made for nothing else. When we live to glorify God, we step into
the only truly humanizing way of living. We function properly, like
a car running on gasoline rather than orange juice. And on top of
that, what more enjoyable kind of life is there? How exhausting is
the misery of self. How energizing are the joys of living for another.

But if the final goal of our lives is to glorify God, what is the way
we get there? Put differently, if we can agree on the "why" of our

lives, can we also agree on the "how"? In what ways do we glorify God? And off into eternity, how will God be glorified forevermore?

One way we glorify God is by our obedience to him, our refusing to believe we know best and instead trusting that his way is the way of life. The Bible calls us to live in an "honorable" way among unbelievers "so that . . . they may see your good deeds and glorify God" (1 Pet. 2:12).

In this final chapter of our study of the heart of Christ I would like to consider one other way that we glorify God, and always will. Jonathan Edwards will be our coach.

———

In a sermon late in life Jonathan Edwards preached: "The creation of the world seems to have been especially for this end . . ."—now, how would you have finished that sentence? Here's how Edwards does:

> The creation of the world seems to have been especially for this end, that the eternal Son of God might obtain a spouse, towards whom he might fully exercise the infinite benevolence of his nature, and to whom he might, as it were, open and pour forth all that immense fountain of condescension, love, and grace that was in his heart, and that in this way God might be glorified.[1]

If you are at all familiar with Edwards, you are likely aware that one of the resounding emphases of his ministry and writing was the

1   Jonathan Edwards, "The Church's Marriage to Her Sons, and to Her God," in *The Works of Jonathan Edwards*, vol. 25, *Sermons and Discourses, 1743–1758*, ed. Wilson H. Kimnach (New Haven, CT: Yale University Press, 2006), 187. Edwards says something very similar in his *Notes on Scripture* after quoting Isa. 62:5. *The Works of Jonathan Edwards*, vol. 15, *Notes on Scripture*, ed. Steven J. Stein (New Haven, CT: Yale University Press, 1998), 187.

glory of God. He was a thoroughly and distinctively God-centered thinker. He wrote a treatise called *The End for Which God Created the World* in which he argued this single point, that the world exists for the glory of God.

But we are sometimes less aware of what Edwards said about *how* this happens. The above quote is a representative statement. God made the world so that his Son's heart had an outlet. We don't use a word like *benevolence* much today; it means a disposition to be kind and good, a crouched coil of compassion ready to spring. Picture a dammed-up river, pent up, engorged, ready to burst forth—that is the kindness in the heart of Christ. He is infinitely benevolent, and human history is his opportunity to "open and pour forth all that immense fountain of condescension, love, and grace." The creation of the world, and the ruinous fall into sin that called for a re-creative work, un-dammed the heart of Christ. And Christ's heart flood is how God's glory surges forth further and brighter than it ever could otherwise.

This marital rapture between Christ and his bride is begun, in relatively small measure so far as our experience goes, in this life. But the final joining of Christ with his bride takes place at the very end of the Bible, as heaven comes down to earth, "prepared as a bride adorned for her husband" (Rev. 21:2). On into eternity we will enjoy the glory of God—but (again) how? The answer is: Christ's glory is preeminently seen and enjoyed in his love to sinners.

The indefatigable and justly famous missionary to Native Americans, David Brainerd, died in the Edwards home in western Massachusetts in October 1747. Jonathan Edwards preached his funeral sermon. Reflecting on seeing Christ in the next life, Edwards said: "The nature of this glory of Christ that they shall see, will be such as will draw and encourage them, for they will not only see infinite

majesty and greatness; but infinite grace, condescension and mildness, and gentleness and sweetness, equal to his majesty." The result
will be that "the sight of Christ's great kingly majesty will be no terror
to them; but will only serve the more to heighten their pleasure and
surprise." More specifically:

> The souls of departed saints with Christ in heaven, shall have
> Christ as it were unbosomed unto them, manifesting those infinite
> riches of love towards them, that have been there from eternity.
> . . . They shall eat and drink abundantly, and swim in the ocean
> of love, and be eternally swallowed up in the infinitely bright,
> and infinitely mild and sweet beams of divine love.[2]

The creation of the world was to give vent to the gracious heart
of Christ. And the joy of heaven is that we will enjoy that unfettered
and undiluted heart forevermore.

———

But is this biblical?

Earlier in our study we considered the phrase "rich in mercy" in
Ephesians 2:4. Have you ever stopped to observe what Paul says, at
the end of that long sentence (v. 7), is the ultimate reason for our
salvation? It goes like this, after delineating our hopeless predica-
ment if left to our own resources:

> But God, being rich in mercy, because of the great love with which
> he loved us, even when we were dead in our trespasses, made us
> alive together with Christ—by grace you have been saved—and

2 Jonathan Edwards, "True Saints, When Absent From the Body, Are Present With the Lord,"
   in *Works*, 25:233.

raised us up with him and seated us with him in the heavenly places in Christ Jesus, so that in the coming ages he might show the immeasurable riches of his grace in kindness toward us in Christ Jesus.

The point of unending eternal life in the new heavens and the new earth is that God "might show the immeasurable riches of his grace in kindness toward us in Christ Jesus."

Here we are. Just ordinary people, anxiously making our way through life, sinning and suffering, wandering and returning, regretting and despairing, persistently drifting away from a heart sense of what we will enjoy forever if we are in Christ.

Does a text like Ephesians 2:7 actually connect with our real-time lives? *Or is it just for the theologians to write about?*

As we close our study of the heart of Christ, I would like to linger over Ephesians 2:7 and consider exactly what we are being liberated into by this short text, which simply reflects Scripture's teaching more broadly on what our future is.

"So that in the coming ages he might show the immeasurable riches of his grace in kindness toward us in Christ Jesus"—what does that mean, for those in Christ? It means that one day God is going to walk us through the wardrobe into Narnia, and we will stand there, paralyzed with joy, wonder, astonishment, and relief.

It means that as we stand there, we will never be scolded for the sins of this life, never looked at askance, and never told, "Enjoy this, but remember you don't deserve this." The very point of heaven and eternity is to enjoy his "grace in kindness." And if the point of heaven is to show the immeasurable riches of his grace in kindness, then we are safe, because the one thing we fear will keep us out—our sin—can only heighten the spectacle of God's grace and kindness.

It means that our fallenness now is not an obstacle to enjoying heaven. It is the key ingredient to enjoying heaven. Whatever mess we have made of our life—that's part of our final glory and calm and radiance. That thing we've done that sent our life into meltdown—that is where God in Christ becomes more real than ever in this life and more wonderful to us in the next. (And those of us who have been pretty squeaky clean will get there one day and realize more than ever how deeply sin and self-righteousness and pride and all kinds of willful subconscious rebellions were way down deep inside us, and how all *that* sends God's grace in kindness soaring, and we too will stand, astonished, at how great his heart is for us.)

If his grace in kindness is "immeasurable," then our failures can never outstrip his grace. Our moments of feeling utterly overwhelmed by life are where God's heart lives. Our most haunted pockets of failure and regret are where his heart is drawn most unswervingly.

If his grace in kindness is "immeasurable *riches*"—as opposed to measurable, middle-class grace—then our sins can never exhaust his heart. On the contrary, the more weakness and failure, the more his heart goes out to his own.

Ephesians 2:7 doesn't just say the "immeasurable riches of his grace" but "the immeasurable riches of his grace *in kindness*." The Greek word for *kindness* means a desire to do what is in your power to prevent discomfort in another. It's the same word used in Matthew 11:30 where Jesus says "my yoke is *easy*." His yoke is kind. On "kindness" in Ephesians 2:7 Goodwin remarks, "the word here implies all sweetness, and all candidness, and all friendliness, and all heartiness, and all goodness, and with his whole heart."[3]

His grace in kindness is "toward us." You could translate this "to us" or even "over us" or "on us." This is personal. Not abstract. His heart, his thoughts, now and on into eternity, are *toward us*. His grace is not a blob out there that we have to figure out how to get into. He sends his grace to us, personally, individually, eternally. Indeed, he sends himself—there's no such "thing" as grace (remembering that such a view is Roman Catholic teaching). He sends not grace in the abstract but Christ himself. That's why Paul immediately adds "in Christ Jesus."

Speaking of "in Christ Jesus," do you realize what is true of you if you are *in Christ*? Those in union with him are promised that all the haunted brokenness that infects everything—every relationship, every conversation, every family, every email, every wakening to consciousness in the morning, every job, every vacation—everything—will one day be rewound and reversed. The more darkness and pain we experience in this life, the more resplendence and relief in the next. As a character says in C. S. Lewis's *The Great Divorce*, reflecting biblical teaching: "That is what mortals misunderstand. They say of some temporal suffering, 'No future bliss can make up for it,' not knowing that Heaven, once attained, will work backwards and turn even that agony into a glory."[4] If you are in Christ, you have been eternally invincibilized. This passage speaks of God making dead people alive, not assisting injured people. And how

3   Thomas Goodwin, *The Works of Thomas Goodwin*, 12 vols. (repr., Grand Rapids, MI: Reformation Heritage, 2006), 2:277.
4   C. S. Lewis, *The Great Divorce* (New York: HarperCollins, 2001), 69.

does he make us alive? "He loves life into us," according to John Owen.[5] His resurrection power that flows into corpses is love itself.

Ephesians 2:7 is telling you that your death is not an end but a beginning. Not a wall, but a door. Not an exit, but an entrance.

The point of all human history and eternity itself is to show what cannot be fully shown. To demonstrate what cannot be adequately demonstrated. In the coming age we will descend ever deeper into God's grace in kindness, into his very heart, and the more we understand of it, the more we will see it to be beyond understanding. It is immeasurable.

For those not in Christ, this life is the best it will ever get. For those in Christ, for whom Ephesians 2:7 is the eternal vista just around the next bend in the road, this life is the worst it will ever get.

> In that resurrection morning, when the Sun of Righteousness shall appear in the heavens, shining in all his brightness and glory, he will come forth as a bridegroom; he shall come in the glory of his Father, with all his holy angels.
>
> That will be a joyful meeting of this glorious bridegroom and bride indeed. Then the bridegroom will appear in all his glory without any veil: and then the saints shall shine forth as the sun in the kingdom of their Father, and at the right hand of their Redeemer.
>
> Then will come the time, when Christ will sweetly invite his spouse to enter in with him into the palace of his glory, which he had been preparing for her from the foundation of the world, and shall as it were take her by the hand, and lead her in with

---

5   John Owen, *On Communion with God*, in *The Works of John Owen*, ed. W. H. Goold (repr., Edinburgh: Banner of Truth, 1965), 2:63.

him: and this glorious bridegroom and bride shall with all their shining ornaments, ascend up together into the heaven of heaven; the whole multitude of glorious angels waiting upon them: and this Son and daughter of God shall, in their united glory and joy, present themselves together before the Father; when Christ shall say, "Here am I, and the children which thou hast given me": and they both shall in that relation and union, together receive the Father's blessing; and shall thenceforward rejoice together, in consummate, uninterrupted, immutable, and everlasting glory, in the love and embraces of each other, and joint enjoyment of the love of the Father.[6]

6   Jonathan Edwards, "The Church's Marriage to Her Sons, and to Her God," in *The Works of Jonathan Edwards*, vol. 25, *Sermons and Discourses, 1743–1758*, ed. Wilson H. Kimnach (New Haven, CT: Yale University Press, 2006), 183–84.

Epilogue

This is a book about the heart of Christ and of God. But what are we to do with this?

The main answer is, nothing. To ask, "Now how do I apply this to my life?" would be a trivialization of the point of this study. If an Eskimo wins a vacation to a sunny place, he doesn't arrive in his hotel room, step out onto the balcony, and wonder how to apply that to his life. He just enjoys it. He just basks.

But there is one thing for us to do. Jesus says it in Matthew 11:28. "Come to me."

Why do we not do this? Goodwin tells us. It's the whole point of our study of Jesus:

> That which keeps men off is, that they know not Christ's mind and heart. . . . The truth is, he is more glad of us than we can be of him. The father of the prodigal was the forwarder of the two to that joyful meeting. Have you a mind? He that came down from heaven, as himself says in the text, to die for you, will meet you more than halfway, as the prodigal's father is

said to do. . . . O therefore come in unto him. If you knew his heart, you would.[1]

Go to him. All that means is, open yourself up to him. Let him love you. The Christian life boils down to two steps:

1. Go to Jesus.
2. See #1.

Whatever is crumbling all around you in your life, wherever you feel stuck, this remains, un-deflectable: his heart for you, the real you, is gentle and lowly. So go to him. That place in your life where you feel most defeated, he is there; he lives there, right there, and his heart for you, not on the other side of it but in that darkness, is gentle and lowly.

Your anguish is his home. Go to him.

"If you knew his heart, you would."[2]

1   Thomas Goodwin, *Encouragements to Faith*, in *The Works of Thomas Goodwin*, 12 vols. (repr., Grand Rapids, MI: Reformation Heritage, 2006), 4:223–24.
2   Goodwin, *Works of Thomas Goodwin*, 4:223.

Acknowledgments

THIS BOOK WOULD NOT EXIST without the following people.

My wife, Stacey. You alone know. Your "adorning [is] the hidden person of the heart with the imperishable beauty of a gentle and quiet spirit" (1 Pet. 3:4).

My brothers, Eric and Gavin, uniquely aware of my sins and struggles, who love me anyway. "Aaron and Hur held up his hands, one on one side, and the other on the other side" (Ex. 17:12).

My dad, Ray, whose life and preaching have convinced me of the heart of Jesus. "Listen to your father who gave you life" (Prov. 23:22).

Drew Hunter, alongside whom I have been reading Goodwin over the past decade, texting each other quotes of discovery about Christ's very heart, astonished together. "I have no one like him" (Phil. 2:20).

Mike Reeves, who introduced me to Thomas Goodwin, whose ministry reflects Goodwin's own heartbeat, and who brings the riches of church history to bear on us today. "Every scribe who has been trained for the kingdom of heaven is like a master of a house, who brings out of his treasure what is new and what is old" (Matt. 13:52).

Art Wittmann, thirty-five years farther along the road of life than I, who through prayer and love is helping me find my way. "The sweetness of a friend comes from his earnest counsel" (Prov. 27:9).

Lane Dennis, my boss, who provided time away to think and write, and who lives and leads Crossway as if God actually exists. "There is laid up for [you] the crown of righteousness" (2 Tim. 4:8).

Crossway colleagues Justin Taylor, Dave DeWit, Lydia Brownback, and Don Jones, who encouraged the book along the way and oversaw its editing and production. "They refreshed my spirit" (1 Cor. 16:18).

The Lord Jesus, the Great-heart. Who could have imagined that you, the most exalted, are the most tender? Meditating on your heart gentleness reduced me to tears more than once as I wrote. Tears of wonder, of relief. "Who then is this?" (Luke 8:25).

General Index

Scripture Index